PLAY
analysis
THE DRAMATURGICAL TURN

Stefano Muneroni

University of Alberta

Kendall Hunt
publishing company

Cover image © Shutterstock, Inc.

Kendall Hunt
publishing company

www.kendallhunt.com
Send all inquiries to:
4050 Westmark Drive
Dubuque, IA 52004-1840

Copyright © 2014 by Stefano Muneroni

ISBN 978-1-4652-4014-9

Printed in Canada
10 9 8 7 6 5 4 3 2 1

Contents

Preface

Writing this book has been a humbling experience for me as I came to realize the numerous influences that have shaped my scholarship and given form to my personal approach to drama. I am indebted to many of my professors who, through the years, taught me how to read plays and passed on to me their wisdom, knowledge of dramatic literature, passion for live theatre and, most importantly, their individual interpretive insights. They taught me that theatre is a profoundly personal experience and that you bring to the reading and watching of plays your own preferences and preconceived notions, as well as the willingness to enjoy an artistic ride over which you have no control. They also imparted to me the belief that the critical analysis of a play must be rigorous and unlock a conversation with the historical past that shaped the play as well as explore the significance of this play in the contemporary world. I must thank them especially for teaching me that there is something empowering in critical reading because readers are intrinsically asked to make decisions: to envision the story, to imagine characters and explore the dramatic potential of their choices, and to visualize how a play might look on the stage today.

I must acknowledge also the many accomplished authors who have written similar books, too many to mention here, and who have guided and inspired my experience of reading plays through their insights and critical acumen. Some of their books I adopted in the play analysis classes I have taught over the course of my career. I have no doubt that some of their ideas resonate in different ways in my book.

This project has developed over the years that I taught play analysis in theatre departments at the University of Pittsburgh, Carnegie Mellon University, and the University of Alberta. I am indebted to the many students I was fortunate to encounter at these institutions and who never failed to inform and transform my own views on drama and theatre. Not only have they helped me to structure the questions I address here, but they have also provided me with an ideal interlocutor. I treasured the in-class discussions as well as the informal conversations we shared, and it is because of these nurturing exchanges that I have decided to address an informal "You" as the ideal reader of this book. It is a collective "You" that encompasses past and future students and that, hopefully, will make the reading more engaging and personal. My ideal reader, to whom I often refer in the book as "reader/dramaturg," is someone who is enrolled in a first- year university class in play analysis and is interested in understanding plays critically. This is an introductory book that I hope will set "you," the student, on a journey of discovery of both play texts and their performances.

Many of the textual examples I use come from plays that I enjoy teaching and the majority are from plays anthologized in Matthew Roudané's *Drama Essentials: An Anthology of Plays*, a book I have adopted for my classes over the past few years.

This is not a prescriptive textbook; it does not pretend to unlock a methodology that works the same way for everybody, nor does it aspire to be exhaustive. There are many such books readily available for interested students. This is simply a pedagogical tool I devised for my classes that arises from my dissatisfaction with the common misconception that play analysis is intrinsically separate from performance. It reflects my academic and practical understanding of production dramaturgy, one that I have developed over many years of personal practice, as well as my own aesthetic and dramaturgical sensibility. As a textbook, it suggests "one" trajectory to the understanding of plays that I hope will be tested and discussed critically in the classroom by inquiring students.

A special thanks to Kim McCaw (University of Alberta) and Dr. Colleen Reilly (Slippery Rock University) for agreeing to talk to me about their work as professional dramaturgs. Their interviews, which can be found at the end of the book, offer an insightful look into the rewarding job of reading and dramaturging plays. I also want to thank Megan Morehouse, my graduate assistant at the University of Alberta, for all her help in getting the manuscript ready for publication, and above all my partner and copyeditor Doug Mertz for his keen eye for detail. Without his help this book would not have been possible.

Introduction

Dramaturgy and Play Analysis

As a dramaturg working on both academic and professional theatre productions over the past ten years, I have developed an appreciation for dramaturgy as a critical methodology to study and stage plays. The choice of connecting the analysis of plays to dramaturgy, a relatively new discipline within the larger field of theatre studies, is relevant for many reasons. Dramaturgy is a totalizing approach that aspires to scrutinize plays in all of their textual and performative dimensions. Not only does dramaturgy focus on the playwright and the play's language, genre, and sociopolitical and cultural conditions, it also concerns itself with what happens to the play when it is finally brought to the stage and is experienced by an audience in the immediacy of performance. Dramaturgy supplies a holistic approach by bridging the gap that separates written drama and live theatre. This book adopts insights from both new-play dramaturgy and production dramaturgy. The former deals with the way a new play evolves into its "final" version through the collaboration between playwright and dramaturg, and sometimes director. This form of dramaturgy deals specifically with forging the text and entails workshops and readings as the primary means to evaluate the performative potential of the script. Production dramaturgy, as implied in its name, assumes that the text is in its definitive version (although changes are possible at this stage as well) and focuses on bringing the text onto the stage. Among their many duties, production dramaturgs assist the director, the designers, and the actors by providing them with much-needed research (historical, cultural, social, etc.) as well as functioning as consultants during the rehearsal process. Both production dramaturgy and new-play dramaturgy are interested in bringing together the solitary work of the playwright with the collective and socially informed one of the creative team. Both also approach plays in their full artistic trajectory, one that demands the realization of the written word in the dialogue spoken by actors, what Brigitte Schultze defines as a journey through "monomedial literature (reading) and polymedial theatre (performance)" (177).

Some of the questions addressed in this book are how can one read a play in a way that fosters a richer imaginative connection to the written text; how can the play text be made to illuminate the contemporary cultural circumstances of the reader/spectator; how one brings the dramatic text to life by unpacking the sociocultural conditions that created that very text in the first place; and how the reader can approach the text as a literary manager and explore how it speaks to specific audiences or communities. In brief, can she/he answer the important question of why a play should be read and staged at this specific moment? This is possibly the most essential question the reader must address as she/he commits to unpacking the complexities of the play and probing its stageability. The urgency that lies at the core of any dramaturg's work is that of justifying a play's worthiness: what makes it relevant to spectators who live in a specific geographical area, in a given historical period, speaking a certain language, and affected by both local and global issues that shape their vision of the world. A reader/dramaturg cannot ignore the basic notion that reading and spectating are activities located within specific sociocultural frames and therefore she/he should ponder thoroughly what it is that makes a play significant and why people might be interested in attending a performance of that play.

It should be evident that examining plays through a dramaturgical frame can foster an understanding of how plays construct and generate meaning. Traditional play analysis teaches one how to interpret a text semantically, how to look at and interpret metaphors, analyze sentence structure and grammar to detect meaning, and probe the depth of characterization to determine motivations and objectives. While this approach has many merits, it is intrinsically tied to literary criticism and looks at plays as textual documents to read and decipher. As such, it fails to fully illustrate the correlation a dramatic text always maintains with live theatre. Plays are written to be performed in front of an audience; therefore, it would be silly to deny the final purpose of a play by only examining it textually.

Another reason to turn to dramaturgy as a tool to read and analyze plays comes from a demand within the field of theatre studies. The face of theatre has changed in the last few decades with the emergence and consolidation of performance studies and the more recent impact of postdramatic theatre. These phenomena shifted the emphasis from the logocentrism of dramatic literature (which focuses on the written text) to the sociality of performance (which concentrates on the theatrical event), and they forced scholars and audiences alike to investigate plays in original ways. Dramaturgy, for its role as connector between the written word and the stage, is in the ideal position to jumpstart a new way to analyze plays.

Reading a play like a dramaturg is a layered and complex experience. Dramaturgs are interested in how a dramatic text fully actualizes itself as a work written by an author in a specific time period, but they also research the play's original and subsequent productions, and its significance for a modern audience. The dramaturg moves comfortably from past to present, from writing to staging to performing, within different sociocultural contexts, languages, genres, and conceptual visions. She/he must be able to thoroughly understand the play and its cultural conditions and transcode that information into a viable sign system that may serve the current production.

How, then, does a dramaturg read a play? What are the skills involved in approaching a play like a dramaturg does? What are the benefits of this approach? Since reading a play is about negotiating what the playwright has provided for you in terms of characterization and circumstances, and your own ability to bring the story to life, dramaturgs must explore both the emotional and dramatic potential of the play. They consider reading to be a critical as well as creative activity in which the reader fleshes out the characters and story in personal terms drawing on previous readings and personal life experiences. Using stage directions, dialogue, and their own inferences about the text and its cultural references, dramaturgs make an effort to "see" the characters in their natural landscape and to "locate" their actions within the spatial reality in which they exist. This approach is both personal and critical as dramaturgs must always interrogate their own reactions to the story while they also critically evaluate the sociocultural aspects of the play. This exercise helps them tune into their own individual and cultural biases and recognize weaknesses in the dramaturgical structure. A meticulous self-analysis, together with solid critical skills, help dramaturgs understand what they like and why, as well as foster their ability to articulate competently their dramaturgical insights.

This very personal approach to the play must expand, eventually, to a more general and critical level. Not only do dramaturgs read the play to get the gist of the story and a sense of the characters' wants, they also pay attention to the specific details of the background story, themes, characters' objectives and relationships, conflicts, climaxes, language, and sociocultural influences. This is the moment at which dramaturgs leave their own feelings and reactions aside and consider the collective values carried by the play and the impact the play might have on a modern audience.

The play is an artifact that has been crafted under very specific cultural influences, but it may have to be delivered to an audience totally unfamiliar with those influences. Dramaturgs look for ways to translate the play's context for a modern audience. It is a daunting task that entails transcultural and intercultural negotiations, as well as strenuous research into the adaptability and marketability of the original story. If the play is from a different era, a dramaturg might reflect on how the playwright might have written the same story today; how cultural values have changed since the time the playwright wrote the play; whether the dramatic piece still speaks to modern sensibilities; whether themes and characters still resonate with a twenty-first century audience; and, ultimately, whether the play is at all culturally relevant. This approach takes the play script out of the solitary act of reading and into the public arena of discussing, critiquing, and watching plays.

A production dramaturg engages in many activities during, and after, multiple readings of a play. She/he will:

- Establish a meaningful relationship with the director from the get-go, and offer her/his availability to brainstorm, do specific research, and share findings.
- Attend production meetings when necessary, and make herself/himself available to the director and designing team from the beginning of the process.
- Consult biographies of the playwright and determine how the play situates itself within her/his larger artistic output: Does this story continue in another play? Do any of the characters appear in other plays by the same author? Would reading one or more of the playwright's works give the dramaturg a better understanding of the play that is being produced?
- If there are multiple editions of the play, consult all of them and read every preface, introductory note, and postface.
- Read all available translations if the play has been translated from another language, especially those used in recent productions.

- Check all geographical and historical references in the play. If necessary, she/he builds a chronology of events and/or a geographical map of the locales and sites described in the play.
- Research the historical time in which the play was composed (historical sources pertinent to the play, as well as politics, religion, etc.)
- Investigate social customs and cultural values of the time in which the play was written.
- Research all references in the play and include them in the dramaturgical package. These may include songs, musical pieces, poems, personages, and events mentioned in the play.
- Create glossaries for foreign or difficult words.
- Verify the pronunciation of archaic or complex words.
- Reflect on how linguistic and stylistic choices communicate the play's genre.
- Investigate how the topics of the play resonated in the public media when the play was first written and staged (original reviews, public responses in books and articles, citations in other plays, censorship, etc.).
- Look into the theatrical history to determine how theatre conventions and acting style might have affected the form and content of the play at the time in which it was first written and produced.
- Research the production history of the play and procure photos and reviews to include in the dramaturgical package.
- Find audio-visual and textual materials that might illuminate aspects of the play such as themes, characters, and given circumstances.
- Ascertain the evidence of modern connections to the play: Does the play echo concerns or discuss issues that are present in contemporary discourses? Locate and document these connections carefully.
- Compile a dramaturgical package to deliver to the director, actors, and designers the first day of rehearsal, containing all the previously listed information.
- Make a public presentation of dramaturgical findings during the first day of rehearsal.
- Attend the first week of rehearsal because that is likely the time when both directors and actors have important

dramaturgical questions. Visit rehearsal when needed in the following weeks.

- Work closely with the marketing office on developing strategies to market the play.
- Find specific groups that might be interested in the play because of their racial, geographical, linguistic, or cultural connections to the story.
- Develop audience engagement activities for specific groups and work closely with the marketing office to target those groups as potential audience members.
- Design outlines, summaries, study guides, or other educational tools to reach out to specific groups attending the performances (for instance, different student populations attending the show to fulfill specific curricular demands).
- Write dramaturgical notes for the program.
- Create lobby displays to introduce the play meaningfully to the general public (exhibits, display of dramaturgical research, installations, etc.).
- Plan and run any talkback following the performances.
- Participate in any post-mortem of the show.
- Hand in the full dramaturgical packet for archival purposes.

The following chapters will address how the dramaturg's skills can promote a more thorough understanding of plays and assist the novice reader in navigating the exciting journey into the world of a play.

CHAPTER 1

The Play

The Overview

I like to believe that starting to read a play, or any other literary work, entails some courtship, a nuanced and studied liaison. Even before opening the book to the first page and starting to read, it is important to take the time to examine the physical appearance of the play itself, because much information can be gathered by this simple activity.

Take a few minutes to think about the title of the play and open up your mind to a creative exploration of what it might mean. Titles are thresholds into the texts, and you want to cross them with great care and attention to facts and clues. The cover can also carry fascinating information because the editor, often in close collaboration with the playwright, is the one who chose it. The cover can tell us what the publishing house perceives as the marketing drive of the play and what aspects of the play it deems most appealing. Consider the use of colors, the type of image, the way the title fits the page, the style and structure of the whole cover, whether the images convey any specific and detectable meaning, whether the images aspire to intrigue the reader into buying the play script, and whether it capitalizes on a catchy title. The cover of the Harper & Row's edition of Peter Shaffer's *Amadeus*, for example, is occupied almost completely by a black figure wearing a mask and stretching his menacing arms toward the observer. The image captures quite literally the moment in the play where a masked Antonio Salieri, pretending to be Death, terrorizes Mozart. Moreover, especially for the reader who knows nothing about the story, it creates an expectation of mystery and horror that could not be farther from the reality of the dramatic story. The picture communicates to the reader the marketing emphasis of the publisher, but in some sense it also implicitly frames her/his experience of the play.

It is common for a cover to show pictures of landmark theatrical productions of the play, or television and cinematic adaptations that brought it to a larger audience. Late editions of Tony Kushner's *Angels in America* capitalize on the iconic image in the HBO movie when Emma Thompson as the Angel comes bursting through the roof and shows herself to Prior, played by Justin Kirk, who is lying in his bed. As the play exists within the cultural landscape that has produced it, the analysis of the cover, however cursory, can provide useful indications of how the play resonates with cultural connotations. As a reader/dramaturg, you want to contextualize this information into your analysis.

Opening the play to the copyright page can also bring about interesting insights. Date of publication, publishing house, and place of publication can all be tools for determining the history of the play. It can inform us whether the play is a translation or an adaptation, and whether it is an acting edition. It provides us with a history of previous editions and it places the publication within an identifiable time period, which a dramaturg might find useful to research further. The place of publication is also relevant as a playwright might have decided to publish her/his play in another country to avoid political backlash, because she/he was in exile, or perhaps just for the cultural cachet given by publishing abroad. This happened to many writers from Fidel Castro's Cuba who managed to avoid censorship by publishing their works abroad after the 1959 revolution, to Spanish writers who moved to Mexico as exiles during the Francisco Franco regime (1939–1975), and to many Mexican playwrights who published in Argentina to gain a larger readership.

The fact that there might be a large number of editions of the play should also alert the reader/dramaturg to possible edits done through the years by the playwright or the editor and invite further philological research into textual variants. If the playwright edited her/his work substantially, the choice of edition becomes important for both readers and audience members as it might invite further reflection on why reading and staging the play is important today.

Read quotes, dedications, prefaces, and acknowledgments very carefully because they can reveal important information about the playwright and her/his work. They can help you comprehend the work's literary landscape and its cultural horizon, as well as the influences that contributed to shaping it. Consider the Theatre Communication Group's edition of Tracy Letts' *August: Osage County*, a riveting and exhilarating play about an Oklahoma family that reunites because of the disappearance of its patriarch, and while waiting, has to come to terms with its dark secrets and traumatic past. The cover of this edition is a picture of the outside of a two-story house at night showing the inside lit up against the darkened exterior. There are no discernable people in the house, as if the place is deserted, and one feels that the warm lights are counteracted by the blackness that surrounds it. Together with the name of the playwright, we see a favorable quote from a New York Times' review, and a gold medallion with the phrase "Winner of the Pulitzer Prize." When you flip through the initial pages, you see the dedication "To Dad," which is quite intriguing given that the play centers around difficult relationships between parents and children. I find myself immediately drawn to the meaning of the dedication and wonder how to use that information in my reading of the play. Even more interestingly, Letts places a long quote from *All the King's Men* by Robert Penn Warren right after the list of characters. This quote is never spoken on stage and serves only to premise the reading of the play script. It is too long to transcribe here in its entirety but here are a few excerpts:

> The child comes home and the parent puts the hooks in him. [. . .] When you get born your father and mother lost something out of themselves, and they are going to bust a hame trying to get it back, and you are it. They know they can't get it all back but they will get as big a chunk out of you as they can. And the good old family reunion, with picnic dinner under the maples, is very much like diving into the octopus tank at the aquarium.

I believe the playwright has included this quote to introduce the characters' predicaments and their desperate attempt to balance their search for autonomy with the ties that bind them to their dysfunctional family. At the same time, he is inviting us to consider how his source, Robert Penn Warren, might be playing a role in his dramaturgical vision of the Weston family. And, in fact, Warren's Pulitzer winning novel delves into complex family relationships, family secrets, and more importantly it portrays the devastating impact the past can have on the future. Tracy Letts places *August: Osage County* within an intertextual territory and encourages his readers to approach his play through their understanding of Warren's *All the King's Men*. This is a textual hint that only the readers get, possibly to help them make sense of the story in the absence of the live performance of the play.

The Playwright

In spite of Roland Barthes' categorical declaration that "the author is dead," the debate over how much a playwright's biography should influence the critical interpretation of her/his play is alive and well. Readers, academics, and critics are still interested in the kind of insights that can be brought to the playwright's work through knowledge of events in her/his life. This can be a valuable tool as long as it does not limit the reader's interpretation: It can help support arguments when needed, but it must disappear when not necessary. It is vital that the reader knows what she/he is looking for, and how the author can either facilitate or hinder the accomplishment of that goal. If the aim of the dramaturg is to establish the cultural significance of a text for a contemporary audience through the detailed analysis of the historical impact the text held in its original emergence, one must also find a way to articulate the role the playwright had in embodying and shaping the cultural content of the original text. In this regard, the playwright becomes quite central as the agent who chose and fashioned characters, topics, styles, and social milieus, as well as the cultural mediator who selected, consciously or not, what to represent of her/his own time and place. The life of the playwright may be reflected in her/his artistic choices and, as such, the dramaturg cannot discard it. While it is essentially true that a work of art, once it is published or staged, enters a cultural and intertextual space of its own and is forever lost to the author, it is also true that the author can be instrumental in unpacking and clarifying the cultural significance of the text, which is the key objective of any dramaturgical research.

Knowing about the playwright brings about an empathetic reaction that can help, and even frame, the reader's response to the play. How do we feel when we read *The House of Bernarda Alba* knowing that the play was published posthumously because its author, Federico García Lorca, was killed for his political ideas by Francisco Franco's militiamen? Does the fact that William Shakespeare's son Hamnet drowned when he was very young influence our reading of Ophelia's death in *Hamlet* as well as how we experience the emotional life of the characters in the play? Would it be productive to abstract Václav Havel's persecution as a political dissident in Soviet Czechoslovakia from his masterpiece *Largo Desolato*? We could clearly ignore all this information and still comprehend and appreciate those plays, but the specific knowledge about their authors enriches our experience by making it personal and relevant. Nevertheless, one of the dangers of accounting for the playwright's biography is that we read into everything that happens in the play and analyze every character through what we know of the author. The dramaturg must be careful to draw on biography only as a strategy to let the play speak more clearly, never to psychologize the characters or trace direct relationships between the author's life and characters in the play. In the drama-turgical process the life of the playwright becomes relevant for the following reasons:

- To contextualize the play within its cultural setting. In this regard, the playwright becomes a tool, one of many, to unpack the play's sociohistorical and cultural scaffoldings.
- To highlight aspects of the play such as character traits and references that might be useful for the production team and performers. While an actor does not need to know that *Long Day's Journey into Night* closely represents Eugene O'Neill's own family, she/he might still find it useful to know about the playwright's background to shape the emotional arc of her/his character.

Given Circumstances

For a dramaturg, understanding the play and sharing her/his knowledge with the production team and performers is the first essential step. Reading a play entails engaging with the given cir-cumstances of the dramatic text. This is a rich and layered exercise that looks at the ways a play generates meaning. The given circum-stances are the conditions of existence of the story, the information that the playwright has decided to include to shape the world of the play. In brief, they are the coordinates that make the play com-prehensible. However, the fact that they are "given" does not nec-essarily mean that they are immediately evident. It takes a careful reading and often more than one, to understand the nature and the impact of the given circumstances on both the plot and the char-acters. The characters' struggle against the given circumstances, or their succumbing to them, is more often than not related to the central conflict of the play; therefore, making sense of the given circumstances is essential to dramaturgical analysis.

Older plays tend to communicate the given circumstances in the exposition at the opening of the play, usually in first scenes, and they function as preparation to the unfolding of the dramatic action and as a framing device for the audience. This dramaturgi-cal tendency will change moderately in the 1700s and then even more drastically at the end of the 1800s with the advent of Modern Theatre, when the background story is delivered throughout the play, interspersed in bits and pieces to generate and keep the spec-tators' attention. William Shakespeare's masterpiece *Hamlet* tells us everything we need to know to understand the background of the story in scene 1 of Act I: the state of affairs in Denmark, the pressing political situation due to the compromised relationship with Norway, the possibility of a military invasion, the new marriage between Gertrude and Claudius and its implications, the melancholic state of Hamlet and his recent return to Denmark, and clearly the introduction of the ghostly figure that will set the whole plot in motion. Misreading this first scene can undermine a full comprehension of the characters' predicaments and what is at stake for them.

What follows is a list of the most common given circumstances and a brief evaluation of their impact on plot and characters.

Place and Time

"Where" and "When" are essential categories to understand the world of the play. A dramaturg conducts careful research into the geographical location of the play and its historical times. This is essential data that helps the actors comprehend their characters' predicaments more organically, informs the director's aesthetics for the production, and supports the designers' vision. Place and time allow us to locate the reality of the play whether we read it or we experience it in the theatre.

While history teaches us of wars, battles, treaties, armistices, and alliances, cultural history provides us with an understanding of how people in different times and places experienced life, related to each other, conceived the family and the state, approached the spiritual world, created a narrative to talk about themselves and their lives, and produced and engaged with the arts. Any given play contains traces of the history that informed it.

As you set out to read a play, write down all historical references that are mentioned in the text and that are relevant to the plot. You will discover that more often than not they affect dramaturgical action and characterization. Conduct some research on the historical facts and people referenced in the play and reflect on their role in shaping the cultural background and the specific situations described. In analyzing *The American Clock*, Arthur Miller's play about the collapse of the American economy following the crash of the stock market in 1929, a dramaturg would compile a list of the numerous historical facts the playwright has woven into the play's fabric to communicate effectively the national despair and widespread loss of faith. As the data grows, a clearer picture of the

United States in the 1920s and 1930s emerges, one that fosters a more detailed narrative for the dramatic trajectory of the characters and that makes clear the sense of social urgency Miller wanted to portray. Drama is not history, clearly, and a dramaturg can never forget that all historical information is only an accessory to inform a more thorough reading of the dramatic action. While she/he should not "over-read" the history in the play, she/he can surely use it to illuminate its impact on the focus, necessity, and drive of the dramatic action. In *The American Clock*, some characters commit suicide, separate from family and friends, and turn to prostitution just to survive. The enormity of these actions appears more understandable and relatable when one examines what happened in the United States during the Great Depression.

Widening the sphere of your research can be an interesting way to gain a sense of historical changes. Check dates and specific references within and without the context of the play to see what was happening in other geopolitical regions at the same time. A synoptic analysis can afford you a simultaneous look at both the local and the global. Knowing the reverberations of the stock market crash on other nations' economies, for instance, helps one comprehend the devastating reality of the characters of *The American Clock*, while at the same time foster a more sympathetic approach to their predicaments. Furthermore, it guarantees a more personal engagement of the reader/spectator who can contemplate critically the local and global impact of politics and economy.

Finally, after you consider the "when" within its historical and cultural manifestations, concentrate also on both the time of year and day in the play. This information can provide a meaningful lens to understand characters' choices and actions.

Geography, the "where" of a play, is important because it relates to cultural values, traditions, and languages. But geography also plays into the reader's cultural expectations and has an effect on how she/he envisions characters and their actions. We would not approach the reading of a play set partially in New York City, such as *Angels in America*, the same way that we would a play such as *Steel Magnolias* that takes place in the southern United States and features more "traditional" family values and a more rustic lifestyle. We do not only approach location through objective knowledge of a specific place, but also through our personal, biased, unsupported, and preconceived notions. This means that the reader/dramaturg should tackle the study of the play's location while at the same interrogating her/his evaluating criteria and biases.

The "where" is also critical due to the influence of climate. Weather affects how characters dress and their clothes conversely determine their physicality; it also impinges on whether they are inside or outside, on where and how they socialize, what they eat and drink, and all other human activities. Derek Walcott, a Nobel prize-winner and a native of the Caribbean island of St. Lucia, depicts characters who are outside most of the time because of where they live. The same thing could not happen in *Bus Stop* by William Inge, where the entire premise of the play is based on the fact that the bus breaks down and the characters have to seek refuge inside a diner because it is too cold outside. In both cases the weather provides the conditions that engender every action the characters take. As you read a play, make an effort to picture what characters wear, how they style their hair, whether it is sunny or rainy outside, if it is cold or hot, whether the season or the month of the year (if the playwright has specified them) influence their behavior, and how they might be engaging the geographical landscape around them. This effort to localize or territorialize the characters and their locales eases the reading of the play by creating long-lasting impressions and memories. This strategy can be extremely helpful if you read the play as an actor who must draw on all pertinent accessory information to motivate her/his character's choices and justify her/his actions.

The "where" of the play is always significant, but it becomes essential in the case of texts that address topical stories where location is essential for comprehending geographically specific themes and characters. As an example, think about the phenomenon of *feminicidio*, the ongoing murders of women in Ciudad Juárez at the border between Mexico and the United States, which has been the topic of many dramas in recent years. These plays invite a political and socioeconomical reading of the setting, and playwrights such as Carlos Morton, Sabina Berman, and Humberto Robles encourage the reader/spectator to look into the reasons why *feminicidio* occurs in this area of the world by pointing at drug wars, globalized economy, and the responsibility of binational policies between the United States and Mexico. It would be virtually impossible to comprehend the predicaments of the characters without understanding first the reality of this region.

Location is relevant in itself but also in how it relates to other locations. When analyzing a play, a dramaturg wants to discover how the play relates to other places around it, and whether there is any crucial connection between places. Understanding the physical distance between Moscow and the rural setting of Anton Chekhov's *Three Sisters* is absolutely necessary to fully comprehend the characters' desperation to return to Moscow as well as the extreme improbability of their return to the capital. It is within this distance that their longing for Russia's cultural center resonates the most. If Moscow were easily accessible, both geographically and financially, the sisters would not desire it so much. A dramaturg would want to research what Moscow might have represented to a person living at the turn of the nineteenth century, and all the cultural attractions available in the city that would have appealed to a young unmarried woman. This information could potentially shed light on aspects of the characters by clarifying the nature of their likes and wants. Even though Chekhov's characters never leave the dreadful military post in the countryside where they reside, understanding the significance of Moscow is essential for unpacking their characters and comprehending their destiny.

Further research into the historical and geographical backdrop of the play can include a deeper look into the architecture, costumes, paintings, decorations, and home interiors for that specific time and place. A dramaturg would include this worthy data in the dramaturgical packet to enhance the visual imagination of the production team and performers and foster an approximation to the world the playwright shaped.

Time and place in nonrealistic plays are just as important. In spite of their not being spelled out or specific in their singular details, space and time are still essential for the reader who must make sense of a story one way or the other. Let's consider Harold Pinter's short one act *Hey Joe!* in which a male character is sitting in an empty room while a female voice retells vague and ambiguous stories about a woman and a house on a beach. While it is unclear where and when the woman's tales take place, the reader knows that the actions happened in an undisclosed past and that these memories carry much pain and trauma. As the narration continues, the voice gets louder and the expression on Joe's face increasingly more desperate. The aseptic and spare room could be anywhere and belong to any time period, as it does not suggest any specific element; however, it is also reminiscent of a hospital room or an insane asylum, images that fit perfectly the general atmosphere of the play. Both time and place are murky but the reader cannot ignore them. They invite a reading that must be even more attentive than in a realistic play because of the virtual absence of clues.

Politics

Reflecting on the impact of political discourse in our world can be an interesting way to approach the relevance of politics in plays. Not only are politics a great source of ideological argument and passionate behavior, they also shape the social environment in which everyone lives. They affect how we relate to the government, perceive individual and collective resources and properties, engage notions of ethics and morals, share cultural and social values, and partake in all civic activities—from voting and electing our leaders, to voicing our dissent. Politics affect every single aspect of our daily life, regardless of whether we are aware of them, but they also solicit and often facilitate personal involvement in the political process, sometimes by asking the individual to acquiesce to the political consensus, in other circumstances by pushing her/him to disagree with the rules and laws of the specific type of government. Politics are active and as such they foster conflict, the very foundation of drama.

For instance, if we do not fully comprehend the role of politics in ancient Greece, we cannot really grasp the reason why Kreon must sentence Antigone to death in Sophocles' *Antigone*. His decision would seem to be the impulsive caprice of a mad tyrant who overreacts to the trifling insubordination of an subaltern being, a woman. A faulty reading of the political circumstances of the play often leads to an easy value judgment where Kreon is the villain and Antigone the heroine. While it is undeniable that our contemporary moral notions make us side with Antigone's quest for justice and her devotion to family, the reality is that the political conditions in Thebes also justify Kreon's decision. The civil war between Eteocles, who defends Thebes, and his brother Polyneices, who is trying to seize power from his uncle Kreon to reinstate the house of Oedipus to the throne, could tear the state apart. Antigone's decision to bury Polyneices against Kreon's will is more than the devoted and righteous act of a sister toward her brother, it also defines itself as a terrorist act against a legitimate ruler at a time in which martial law has been decreed to protect the citizenry. This may sound tyrannical and unlawful to a modern audience, but it would have made perfect sense in ancient Greece where war was a real possibility and rulers often had to respond to internal and external opposition in violent ways. Since the civil war is not over and there is still a real danger of another armed insurrection, Antigone's defiance must be contextualized within an explosive political reality:

No, from the very beginning
There have been those who have whispered together,
Stiff-necked anarchists, putting their heads together,
Scheming against me in the alleys. These are the men,
And they have bribed my own guards to do this thing.

While treason is the primary reason for Antigone's death sentence ("Her mind's a traitor's"), her sedition is another damning allegation because it opens up the very real possibility of a widespread and disastrous rebellion ("But how much worse than this / Is brazen boasting of barefaced anarchy"). The crime of burying her brother is worsened by Antigone's open justification of her act, which has the potential to turn her into a political leader for the dispersed forces that had supported Polyneices' quest for the throne. It is not surprising that Kreon mentions this possibility later on when talking to Ismene: "Snake in ordered house, sucking my blood / Stealthily –and all the time I never knew / That these two sisters were aiming at my throne!" Antigone's shift from family member to political opponent, at least in Kreon's perception, is what we need to ponder if we are to comprehend the rich dramaturgical reverberations of the play, the balanced antagonisms between family and state, and the layered imbrication of individual and collective values that Sophocles has given us.

When plays are not directly addressing political issues, detecting the role of politics can be a little harder and might take further research on the part of the reader/dramaturg. In Suzan-Lori Parks' *Topdog/Underdog*, Lincoln, an African American man, works in an arcade where he is paid to reenact the final moments of Abraham Lincoln's life. He sits in the dark and waits for paying customers to shoot him as he pretends to be President Lincoln attending the theatre with his stovepipe hat and his face painted white. Parks plays with the idea of Lincoln, as the recognized antislavery president, and questions the way history is transmitted and the metaphorical racial implications of playing such a role. The playwright prefaces the play with a brief passage describing how this ongoing conversation between past and present occurs through the relationship between a present-day Lincoln and his brother Booth, who carries the same name as John Wilkes Booth, the assassin of

President Lincoln. While Parks gives the reader enough information to understand the relevance of the historical Abraham Lincoln in the unfolding of the characters' trajectory, additional research could enrich the analysis of the play and lead to a more critical understanding.

Just as a dramaturg moves comfortably from the original text to the possible significations of that text in a modern day production, the reader/dramaturg should interrogate how the play can help shed light on current political issues. What is it that we can learn from reading and staging *Antigone* or *Hamlet* today? Can we draw direct connections between what happens in the play and what happens to us daily? Even when the parallelisms are not evident, can one think of another cultural or sociopolitical reality where such conditions manifest themselves? Finally, if the original text's cultural content reactivates itself within our modern sensibility, what do we learn that we did not know before? What moral lessons, humanistic truths, or cultural values do we learn as we reflect on the similarities and differences between the original play (source text) and its staging today (target text)? Answering these and similar questions can open up a meaningful dialogue about the exchange and passing of cultural contents and contexts happening when we read and stage theatre.

Economy

Another crucial aspect that must be studied in correlation with the political landscape of the play is the economic system in which characters live. Economy speaks not only to wealth, class, and status, it also draws on ideological and political values, formation and maintenance of social hierarchies, and characters' understanding of class consciousness and personal worth. It would be hard to ignore the connection between politics and economy when reading a play like *Death of a Salesman*. The American Dream that Willy Loman has internalized and that has caused his distorted sense of self and his idealization of the salesman is the direct result of postwar American politics and its accompanying capitalistic economic system. These two forces are so powerful together that they lead Willy to "have the wrong dream," as Biff claims at the end of the play. By the same token, one can argue that Biff is also completely imbued in the political and economic landscape of the play but that he fights against it. The ideologies sustaining politics and economy are usually intertwined, as in many British plays where the division between the upper and lower classes is derived from the aristocratic system and results in different labor and living conditions, salaries, and life expectations.

A productive way to interrogate the relationship between politics and economy is to determine where, and on what, "value" is to be placed in the play. The reader/dramaturg must discover value in its most basic meaning: what characters desire and fight for; what they consider worthy; what they are willing to sacrifice to acquire the valued objects; what forces or characters either enable them to obtain what they want, or hinder their efforts; what bureaucratic and official channels generate a collective perception of value; and whether the state is responsible for buttressing and protecting what characters perceive as valuable. *Death of a Salesman* is exemplary from this point of view because in this play everything comes with a price tag: the life insurance, the mortgage, the loan Biff should ask from Bill Oliver, the salary increase Willy demands from Howard, the price of repairs and the purchase of single items, the money Charley lends Willy every month, and so on. The sheer accumulation of dollar amounts tells us more than what the characters need to survive. It informs us how money defines their image of themselves. Willy takes money from Charley under the pretext of a loan but cannot bring himself to work for Charley because he perceives that as humiliating. When Willy tries to convince Howard to let him work in New York, he only asks for $40, a small sum for a family in the 1940s, a fact that mirrors both his diminished sense of self as well as his growing desperation. Finally, when Biff wants to ask Oliver for $10,000, Willy advises him to ask for $15,000, not only because it's a larger amount but also for the respect that asking for and receiving more money carries. The higher sum Willy suggests comes after a series of remarks about Biff's supposed boyish behavior ("Don't crack any jokes," "Walk in very serious," "Everybody likes a kidder, but nobody lends him money," "And don't say 'Gee. Gee is a boy's word. A man walking in for fifteen thousand dollars does not say 'Gee!' Don't be so modest." Roudané 379–381). This is a clear indication of how money represents a viable way to communicate aspects of the characterization in a nuanced and fluid way. The possession of "value" frames the given reality of the characters and shapes their own perception of themselves and their relationship with other characters.

Together with politics, economy is one of the most impacting given circumstances and the dramaturg/reader should analyze it thoroughly in the specific context of the play. Fifteen thousand dollars was clearly a large sum of money in the 1940s and could have easily guaranteed the success of the "Loman Brothers" enterprise that Happy dreamed of starting with his brother Biff. However, it does not communicate the true value of the loan unless we convert that amount into contemporary dollars and imagine the impact such a sum would have on our lives today.

Religion

Just like politics, religion shapes human behavior and affects both personal and collective choices. It creates a narrative to read the human experience vis-à-vis the presence of divine being(s); it provides a view of the future and sometimes of the afterlife; it codifies ethics and morals; it establishes a system of rewards and penalties for behavior; and it impacts enormously our views on gender, sex, and politics. One could reasonably argue that religion is a powerful force even in its absence, as atheism implies a view of religion just as strong as fundamentalism. A dramaturg should analyze the role of religion in drama both when it is overtly present as well as when it is couched subtly within the plot and characterization. For instance, it would be impossible to miss the relevance of religion in a mystery play from the British cycles of the Middle Ages, or in a Jesuit college play from the seventeenth century because religion sits at the very core of these types of drama. However, it might be more difficult to detect religion's role in a play like *Hamlet* where theological and spiritual concerns are less evident. When Hamlet finds Claudius kneeling and praying, he claims

> Now might I do it [pat], now'a is a-praying;
> And now I'll do't –and so'a goes to heaven,
> And so am I [reveng'd]. That would be scann'd:
> A villain kills my father, and for that
> I, his sole son, do this same villain send
> To heaven.
> Why, this is [hire and salary], not revenge.
> 'A took my father grossly, full of bread,
> With all his crimes broad blown, as flush as May,

And how his audit stands who knows save heaven?
But in our circumstance and course of thought
'Tis heavy with him. And am I then revenged,
To take him in the purging of his soul,
When he is fit and season'd for his passage?
No! (Roudané 147)

From the above passage we understand Hamlet's hesitation to kill because of his belief in the afterlife, a notion that makes the hero's later choices even more significant. How does Hamlet feel about murdering Claudius, knowing it is an act condemned in the Bible? Does he believe he will be damned forever? Can his religious sentiments help us understand his tormented and divided self as he is caught between what is expected of him as son and his personal beliefs? Religion is not merely a pretext for delaying the tragic deed, what many critics have deemed Hamlet's indecision, but is an essential circumstance that should inform our reading of the whole play.

A play can also be rich in religious images that may or may not be used to espouse specific religious beliefs. Tony Kushner's *Angels in America* draws heavily on both the Christian and Jewish faiths to discuss queer and political issues in Ronald Reagan's America. Terence McNally revisits the crucifixion to probe similarities between Christ's passion and gay bashing in *Corpus Christi*. In his 1958 play *JB*, Archibald MacLeish reverts to the Biblical story of Job to debunk the original narrative and suggest mankind's emancipation from a voluble and capricious God as a truly humanistic epiphany. Those plays, and many others, use religion both as a trope to transform and adapt stories that are well-known to the general public, as well as a dramaturgical strategy to shape character and plot.

Gender and Sex

Any play represents a given cultural context and as such it describes social relationships within a horizon of expectations. Characters live within these expectations and may conform to or oppose them. Sometimes the dramatic conflict relates specifically to refuting or debunking what society expects of them. A contextual analysis of gender and sexual roles is essential to fully comprehend characters' motivations, objectives, aspirations, and desires. Antigone's defiance of the law takes on a cultural connotation specifically because she is a woman who, according to ancient Greek standards of conduct, should abide by male rule and, more specifically, abstain from questioning the decision of the monarch. Her open rebellion brings up a more insidious threat for Kreon because if a woman can defy him, then anybody can. Another classical example of female identity and its centrality to the dramatic action is Medea from Euripides' homonymous play. Medea is every man's worst nightmare because she not only rebels against patriarchal rule, she also destroys her male partner by murdering his progeny, thus depriving him of both immediate happiness and any potential future. As a non-Greek person, a barbarian, Greek society endows her female identity with other dangerous traits such as uncontained passions, witchcraft, and foreign allegiances. The fact that her numerous negative qualities coalesce around Medea's gender is something one cannot miss while reading this tragedy. As every play, to some extent, portrays and reiterates sexual and gender expectations, it is absolutely important to understand how the playwright has codified these elements to shape the reality of the characters and the trajectory of the dramatic action. Unpacking the specific relevance of sex and gender in the original play is a preliminary step in making sense of its modern reading and staging. There are countless adaptations of the Medea trope that explore new dramaturgical possibilities for this character, from a strictly feminist perspective to a postcolonial and intercultural point of view. As notions of sex and gender evolve, one should negotiate with the past to understand how it can still signify in the present.

Cultural notions of sex and gender are always present even when the playwright does not explicate them or delve directly into their social impact. Consider Linda in *Death of a Salesman*, a wife who represents completely the standards of the post-WWII woman by tolerating her husband's verbal abuse and overlooking all of his faults. While this is not the central aspect of Miller's play, it is indeed an important thing to consider because Linda functions as the moral compass of the story and allows the reader to reflect on the formation of Cold War masculinities. With her respectful yet assertive conduct, Linda is the epitome of 1950s' female exemplary manners while at the same time offering a significant commentary on masculine behavior. Her strong influence on both Willy and her sons, Biff and Happy, can hardly be overlooked.

Sex and gender are essential categories in plays that address specifically shifting configurations of cultural norms. The appearance of plays dealing with gay characters and themes such as those in *Angels in America*, *Jeffrey*, *The Boys in the Band*, and *A Normal Heart* would not have been possible without the Stonewall Riots, the pro-liferation of gay activism in the 1970s and 1980s, and the AIDS epi-demic. By the same token, a play like *Diana of Dobsons* by Cicely Hamilton, a play about women entering the workspace and fight-ing for basic civil rights, could hardly make sense without studying the suffragette movement and cultural shifts in the perception of family and gender roles in Britain in the 1800s.

Characters' Given Circumstances

Take note of all the indications the playwright has given you about characters. These are both important clues to locate the characters within the specificity of their world and effective tools for compre-hending their objectives and motivations. Consider carefully the characters' age, sex, education, wealth and status, race and ethnic-ity, geographical location, living conditions, political and religious views. These observations will tell you a lot about the characters to be sure, but do not stop there. Consider what they read, eat, and like to do; what they say about themselves; their likes and dislikes; how they address and speak to/about other characters, and how other characters relate to and speak about them. In brief, try to dis-cover as much as you can about them so that you may understand their dramatic wants, as well as the source of these wants. Your role as reader/dramaturg is similar to that of a private detective who is studying his subject to compile a profile full of significant details that might help explain the subject's life choices and future.

Arthur Miller does not tell us much about Biff in *Death of a Sales-man*, but the few things he does say are relevant to understand the character better: Biff is good-looking, he is in his thirties, and he likes to work outside. His looks speak to his success with women and the self-confidence he displayed in the past (how he related to his childhood friend, Bernard), and to the fact he was well-liked by people (the cohort of worshippers he always had around while growing up, and his promise of being a successful athlete). His age indicates that there is a discrepancy between what he has achieved and what he should/could have accomplished in his life. It also makes Willy's continued dreams of glory for Biff quite delu-sional. Our perception of Biff, and of his relationship with Willy, would be clearly different if he were an average-looking teenager living at home. Finally, the fact that he likes to do physical work and be outside immediately sets up a difference with Willy, whose work as a salesman deals with an urban setting and office skills.

By researching carefully Biff's given circumstances, you can access a more thorough comprehension of the character's decisions and his relationship with other characters in the play.

Theatrical History

When analyzing the play script, a dramaturg must research the theatrical history that shaped the piece. The text reflects the theatrical conditions of the time, including how playwrights understood and crafted dramatic action and character, chose specific styles and genres over others, opted for suitable topics according to well-established moral and social principles, and reflected the commonly accepted sociocultural values of their time. The text also reflects the inherent boundaries of the theatrical facilities and acting styles of the time. Familiarize yourself with the theatrical advancements in acting, design, direction, and dramaturgy at the time in which the play was written so as to be able to find clues as to why characters speak and act the way they do. Explore how changes in theatre buildings and stage techniques affected the development of play scripts. What is the connection between the introduction of gas lighting in the theatre and the way playwrights started to compose their plays? What are the dramaturgical consequences of actresses breaking the male monopoly on acting and making their triumphant entrance onto the English stage at the time of the Restoration? How did the translation of Aristotle's *Poetics* affect play writing and reception of Renaissance and Neoclassical dramas? How did the emergence of public theatres affect the kind of stories playwrights began to tackle? Those are just a few questions to get you thinking about the different levels of analysis you should engage in while reading a play. A good theatre history book can be an excellent tool to appreciate the play in its context and enjoy all its cultural nuances.

As an example, the development and success of *commedia dell'arte* throughout Europe between the sixteenth and the eighteenth centuries makes a lot more sense once you consider the material conditions and conventions of theatre at the time. These comedians represented an alternative to the boring theatre produced by the academies and the court, which was inaccessible to most spectators. The performers of *commedia dell'arte* had fewer technical requirements and were able to perform both indoors and out. They appealed to a larger audience because they were among the first to introduce actresses on stage and chose topics that were intriguing and saucy. Finally, they were true professionals who innovated the medium of theatre through their scenarios, character types, use of masks, and *lazzi*. Looking at a scenario anthologized by Flaminio Scala in 1611 will not tell you much about *commedia dell'arte* unless you are willing to delve deeper into the research of style and conventions of this movement.

Practicum

Consider the following "open scene," an ambiguous dialogue that can be interpreted in different ways according to the given circumstances that are chosen to justify it. It is a very short scene with only two characters: A and B. Use clues within the text, as well as your imagination to answer the following questions:

1. Decide what it is that the scene represents. What do the characters argue about? What is the conflict? What are the dramatic stakes in the scene? What is it that "must be delivered"?
2. Establish the relationship between A and B. Are they related? Do they have a business relationship? Do they live together?
3. Find out what is it that A and B want, together and individually.
4. Make sure you determine characters' sex, age, profession, race, education, and political and religious views.
5. Picture the characters in as many details as you possibly can: height, weight, eye/hair color, clothes, accessories, and other features.
6. Determine when the scene takes place (contemporary time? What time of the year, or the day, is it? Is it cold or hot?).
7. Establish where the scene takes place (nation, city, type of neighborhood).
8. Envision the specific details of the space where the scene takes place. Is it outside or inside? Is it a house or an apartment? What room is it? How is it decorated? Does it have windows? What can you see outside?
9. After you have done the exercise one time, try changing the given circumstances to envision the dramatic action and the characters in a completely different way.
10. Reflect also on how the dialogue changes completely its significance once the given circumstances change.

The Delivery

A: Where you been?
B: Out . . . and about . . .
A: Nice for you . . . Did you deliver it?
B: No.
A: Why do contradict me all the time, eh? I'm so . . .

B: What? Tired?

A: Fed up, that was my word. But tell me why I shouldn't be tired too.

B: Sure, you can be all these things. Knock yourself out . . . Happy?

A: No, you?

B: Whatever.

A: Don't you . . .

B: I'll do it tomorrow, OK? Maybe the rain will let up . . .

A: Don't miss the bus. I ain't paying for the fuckin' taxi again.

B: OK.

A: It'd better be OK.

B: I said it's OK, what else do you want from me?

A: I want you to do your job, that's all!

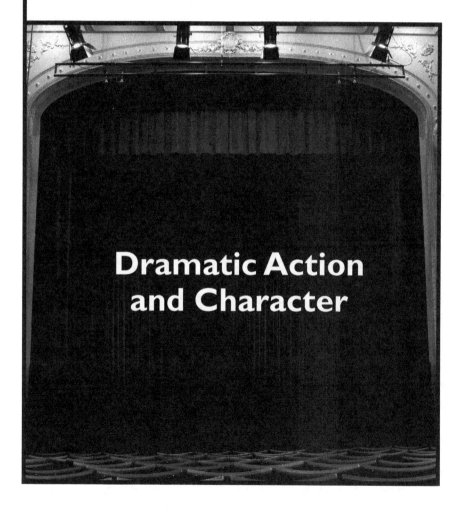

CHAPTER 2

**Dramatic Action
and Character**

Dramatic Action

Aristotle's *Poetics* is still the most important text in dramaturgical theory, and the one that has had the greatest impact on how playwrights write plays and readers interpret them. This fourth-century B.C.E. treatise was rediscovered and popularized during the Renaissance thanks to numerous translations, which not only made readily available the ideas of the Greek philosopher but also misinterpreted some of them. For instance, the widespread belief that Aristotle discusses the three unities of action, time, and place is a common mistake, and so is the belief that the audience is central to Aristotle's critical text. In reality, Aristotle addresses only the unity of action and is interested solely in the mechanics of plays. In spite of these misunderstandings, however, the *Poetics* has established itself as the unavoidable must-read for all theatre students and continues to generate lively academic discourse and much critical literature about plot structure and character.

A dramaturg's approach to a play she/he is researching for a production is quintessentially Aristotelian in that it entails the careful analysis of the six categories Aristotle discussed as central to tragedy: plot, character, thought, diction, music, and spectacle. This is clearly the most essential part of the dramaturg's job because she/he must understand and communicate to the director and production team how the play works as a structure (plot); must provide the performers with ways to understand their roles, both historically and in the present time (character); must justify and explicate what the play intends to signify, its moral and ethical trajectory (thought); must examine the language of the play and clarify its linguistic, semantic, and cultural meanings (diction); must evaluate and illustrate the role of harmony, melody, and song (music); and finally must explore the suitability of specific design elements to the play script (spectacle). Dramaturgs rely heavily on Aristotle's critical ideas to investigate a play. As a tool, the *Poetics* provides the researcher with precious insight about how to read a play and make sense of it. Although what remains of the *Poetics* addresses mainly the genre of tragedy, some of the critical lessons it provides, specifically those of emplotment and dramatic action, can find an application in all theatrical genres.

Aristotle claims that the foundation of tragedy is set in "action," and he phrases his belief in the following terms:

> Tragedy is essentially an imitation not of persons but of action and life, of happiness and misery. All human

happiness or misery takes the form of action; the end for which we live is a certain kind of activity, not a quality. Characters give us qualities, but it is in our actions—what we do—that we are happy or the reverse. In a play accordingly they do not act in order to portray the Characters; they include the Characters for the sake of the action. (Gerould 50)

It is necessary to unpack the meaning of "activity" versus "quality" if we are to understand what Aristotle meant by action. Quality is a trait or attribute that a playwright uses to describe a character or situation, but it does not suggest the act of doing something, nor does it describe anything universal or totalizing. For instance, Hamlet is melancholic but that quality alone does not define him; it is simply one quality among many others he has and displays. Moreover, a quality does not imply an activity (a state of doing) but simply an attribute or trait (a state of being). While a quality can be highly appealing from many points of view, it lacks the directness of the action and points inwardly toward the subject instead of outwardly toward the object of the action. The Merriam-Webster dictionary of the English language describes the verb "to act" as "1a: the doing of a thing: DEED b: something done voluntarily 2: a state of real existence rather than possibility [. . .] 4: the process of doing: ACTION." (12) These meanings point in the direction of a subject who completely commits to an activity and they presuppose the total presence of the subject in the actions she/he executes. To act, in this regard, means that the character is manifesting her/his desires openly by performing acts and thus changing the reality around her/him. It also suggests that the subject executing the action willingly extends her/himself into the world and that her/his actions will be predicated on an object. In brief, actions always carry consequences; they transform reality and shift our perception of the world. That does not necessarily mean that actions always carry physical movement, but rather that a dramatic action has always the potential to make a difference, regardless of whether the action is physical, verbal, or silent.

Aristotle emphasizes the key role that action plays in drama, arguing that although tragedy can exist without characters, it could never exist without action. For this reason, it is crucial to understand the central role actions play in drama and how they can unlock our understanding of theatre.

To avoid the risk of either missing pivotal dramatic actions altogether, or concentrating on minor actions that do not carry special significance, it is important to pay close attention to textual and extra-textual clues:

- Take notice of what the stage directions communicate about exits and entrances, and/or of anything characters do that is not immediately delivered by dialogue.
- Check to see if the characters are describing any actions.
- Reflect on actions that have happened offstage but affect the onstage reality.

Consider the scene of *Antigone* in which Kreon finds out that both his son and wife are dead and think about the types of action described:

MESSENGER: She stood before the altar, and her heart welcomed the knife her own hand guided, and a great cry burst from her lips for Megareus dead, and for Haimon dead, her sons; and her last breath was a curse for their father, the murderer of her sons. And she fell, and the dark flowed in through her closing eyes.

KREON: O God, I am sick with fear. Are there no swords here? Has no one a blow for me?

MESSENGER: Her curse is upon you for the deaths of both.

KREON: It is right that it should be. I alone am guilty. I know it, and I say it. Lead me in, quickly, friends. I have neither life nor substance. Lead me in.

CHORAGUS: You are right, if there can be right in so much wrong. The briefest way is best in a world of sorrow.

KREON: Let it come. Let death come quickly, and be kind to me. I would not ever see the sun again.

CHORAGUS: All that will come when it will; but we, meanwhile, have much to do. Leave the future to itself.

KREON: All my heart was in that prayer!

CHORAGUS: Then do not pray anymore: the sky is deaf.

KREON: Lead me away. I have been rash and foolish. I have killed my son and my wife. I look for comfort; my comfort lies here dead. Whatever my hands have touched has come to nothing. Fate has brought all my pride to a thought of dust.

(*As Kreon is being led into the house, the CHORAGUS advances and speaks directly to the audience*)

CHORAGUS: There is no happiness where there is no wisdom; no wisdom but in submission to the gods. Big words are always punished, and proud men in old age learn to be wise. (Roudané 72–73)

This scene holds a lot of clues about dramatic action. The messenger's speech about the suicide of Eurydice is a list of single actions that powerfully describe the last moments of her life: She stands, stabs herself, cries, curses her husband, falls, and dies. The chronology of the event is delivered through short sentences and simple punctuation, mostly commas. Although the suicide happens offstage, as was customary in Greek theatre, the recollection of the events still carries dramatic action. The words of the messenger allow the spectators to imagine the tragic end of the queen, whose body is presently displayed on stage thanks to the *ekkykleuma*, the rotating platform that showed the results of violent action that occurred offstage. Kreon's response is one of sheer desperation, suggesting an altered state of mind, and it is feasible to envision him going around the stage asking people in the Chorus for a sword, and urging them to kill him. His following line—"It is right that it should be"—shows his painful acceptance of his responsibility in the demise of his household, and it appears to convey the image of a defeated king who might be possibly kneeling. His request to be taken inside the house falls on deaf ears as no one wants to listen to him or help him. Kreon is now carrying *miasma*, the Greek moral and physical pollution that separates him from the rest of the community. Following the text's clues, one can picture Kreon in this subdued position for the remaining part of the scene. In fact, he claims that his comfort, Eurydice, "lies here dead," thus he is close to her body, center stage, in what is possibly the most striking stage position at this moment of the play. The stage directions indicate that Kreon is finally brought inside as the Choragus comes forth to deliver the last lines of the play. The play, however, provides us also with a sense of future actions as Kreon has informed us that he "would not see the sun again," a statement that might allude to his incipient suicide or that, even more poignantly, reminds us that Kreon's destiny will be similar to the one he had decreed for Antigone: a live burial. The example above illustrates that analyzing the actions in a play should entail both a keen eye for textual indications as well as the creativity and imagination to determine actions that the playwright might have couched in the language or simply implied by the context of the play.

Actions do not exist in a vacuum. They always stem from and feed into other actions, so it is paramount that when you investigate a character's action, you contextualize it within a chain of actions so to establish with enough certainty the super-objective of the character, a concept that is explained later.

Story versus Plot

While the story of a play follows a chronological development and accounts for all the details that are comprised in the narrative of the story, plot speaks to how the playwright presents the episodes of the story to create the play as we know it, and how she/he "picks and chooses" what segments of the story to include. Plots do not have to be chronological and do not necessarily follow a cause-effect structure. Rather, they organize how the story is told; they display carefully crafted scenes so as to fully exploit the dramatic potential of the story; and they arrange the scenes so that characters emerge as affective and dramatic, both transformed and transformative. Consider Harold Pinter's *Betrayal*, a play about adultery and the dissolution of a marriage that takes place over a span of nine years but is told in reverse chronological order. The plot begins with the dissolution of the marriage and ends with the initiation of the affair between Emma, the wife, and Jerry, her husband's best friend, which caused the marriage to fail. Pinter has chosen to start the plot with the very end of the story.

Aristotle considered plot the most important of his six elements of tragedy, and categorized plots as simple or complex according to their structure, their probability and universality, and their inclusion of secondary storylines. When you read a play, make sure you dedicate time and effort to research how the playwright has crafted the story: dramaturgical structure, dramatic trajectory, use of obstacles and conflicts to enhance the dramatic impact of the play, and placement and function of climax(es) and denouement. The emplotment shapes not only how the story is told, but also how the characters fare in the play. Plot and character are brought together by the very notion of action.

Theme versus Super-objective

Now that we have identified the crucial role of dramatic action and explored a few ways to detect and study it, we will consider how actions relate to the analysis of character. As mentioned earlier, dramaturgs must understand characters just as well as actors do because characters are the vessels through which actions manifest themselves, and also because characters are the major affective element in a play. We might miss a few details of the story, or might not understand some of the sociocultural aspects, but most likely we will latch onto something in one or more of the characters. By the same token, when we go to the theatre we might enjoy the directorial vision and the design, but it is unlikely that we are going to express an overall positive judgment on the show if the characters were uninteresting, or even worse, if the actors failed to do justice to the characters' dramatic potential. As readers and audience members, we tend to project ourselves onto characters in a fashion that is both empathetic and emotional.

As you read a play the first time, follow the directions Constantin Stanislavski gave his students in *An Actor Prepares* for approaching the study of dramatic action in a play. In what is possibly one of the most relevant theatre books of the past two centuries, Stanislavski laments the lack of skill some actors showed in play analysis and advised his students to follow a simple rule:

> Do not break up a play more than it is necessary, do not use details to guide you. Create a channel outlined by large divisions, which have been thoroughly worked out and filled down to the last detail. The technique of division is comparatively simple. You ask yourself: "What is the core of the play—the thing without which it cannot exist?" Then you go over the main points without entering into details. [. . .] You have divided the play into its main organic episodes, its largest units. Now draw from each of these units its essential content and you will have the inner outline of the whole play. Each large unit is in turn divided into the medium and small parts which, together, compose it. (Stanislavski 109–110)

Stanislavski invites us to consider how the larger design or principal idea of the play should be the guiding principle for anyone reading a play for meaning. One must understand what it is that the play means as an organic whole: what formal qualities shape this play into what it is, its very reason to be. Stanislavski is not talking here about the theme, which also describes what the play is about but does so by drawing on less active and binding language. The Russian director is addressing instead what is commonly discussed as the super-objective of a play, which differs from the theme in that it is more active. For instance, if *Antigone*'s theme is "the difficulty to abide by both family and state laws," its super-objective would be "to protect Thebes." The super-objective describes the principal idea of the play in a way that suggests action, a move forward. The theme, on the other hand, designates a shift from individual to universal experience and explains some philosophical understanding of the play's world. Stanislavski suggests that once the student has identified the play's main idea, she/he divides the play into sections and determines for each of them what the objective is and how it relates to the main idea of the play. The student should then dissect each section into smaller segments and reflect on how they relate to both the larger sections and the main idea. This fragmentation of the text is only temporary, says Stanislavski, as the text will have to be put back together; however, it is a necessary exercise to fully understand the play and the characters in it.

As a matter of fact, the super-objective describes not only a quality of the play but is also a critical tool for understanding the dramatic arc of each character: "In a play the whole stream of individual, minor objectives, all the imaginative thoughts, feelings and actions of an actor, should converge to carry out the *super-objective* of the plot" (Stanislavski 256). For all of the major characters, but especially for the protagonist and antagonist, make sure you take notice of what their most important "want" is. This is their character's super-objective, the one "wish" that conditions and justifies all their other objectives. Antigone wants to bury her brother because she loves him dearly, and this is her objective; however, she also wants to uphold the laws of the gods without whose protection Thebes would be in danger, and this is ultimately her super-objective. Her major preoccupation coincides with the civic mission of Greek theatre, which considered the stage a tool to inform and educate the citizens of the *polis*. Once you have located the super-objective of the character, trace and possibly underline all the actions that you identify as being related to the super-objective. Each of these actions will convey single objectives that are in some way or form connected to the super-objective. Try picturing these objectives as active verbs to preserve their dynamic nature.

One must discriminate between objectives and motivations to fully comprehend what characters want and how they go about achieving what they desire. While a motivation is something that underlies the character's objective, sometimes in very subtle and unconscious ways, the objective is a clear statement of intent that always carries some action. Make sure you discriminate between the two because misunderstanding their different roles can lead to a wrongful interpretation of the play as a whole.

Conflict

When characters want different things, their objectives clash, thus producing conflict. Conflict can arise within a character (person versus self), between characters (person versus person), between character and family, society, political establishment, sociocultural institutions (person versus environment), and between character and faith or destiny (person versus the spiritual world). More often than not, a character will have to fight one or more of these battles simultaneously. Think of Hamlet, who is struggling against himself as he tries to decide when and how to revenge his father, while he is also managing to find the courage to embrace murder as a viable solution. He also struggles against Claudius as the ruling king of Denmark, against his mother Gertrude's decision to remarry so soon, and against the whole court that is now supporting his uncle. Ultimately, you could argue that Hamlet is also struggling with God, who allowed pain and violence, and finds himself conflicting with a vision of the world he cannot understand. While this last conflict informs all of the others, as a dramaturg and play reader you should avoid generalization and you should always start your analysis from the objective and evident conflicts.

Dramatic conflict is profoundly tied to opposing views about the world and its reverberations are felt not only in the entire play but also in its theatrical rendition on stage. A play without a strong conflict can be quite boring and consequently fail to engage both readers and playgoers. The dramatic conflict shapes how a reader/ dramaturg envisions the characters and the world of the play, and also affects directorial and designing choices. Consider, for instance, the cinematic rendition of *Antigone* directed by Don Taylor, and performed by Juliet Stevenson, John Shrapnel, and John Gielgud.

Here the conflict between state and family values finds its visual representation in stark and militaristic costumes, a set that portrays the court as monumental and stifling, and gigantic pictures of the king resembling an angry Benito Mussolini. While Kreon looks and acts like a power-thirsty tyrant, Antigone is dressed simply but decorously, and sports long hair and an innocent look that shows both her young age and naiveté. The movie takes a firm stance with regard to the representation of the play's conflict and invites the spectator to side with Antigone from the very first moment. The director evidently saw Antigone's argument as stronger than Kreon's and made the important decision to construct her as the innocent victim fighting against the impossibly authoritative rule of an unlawful dictator. As a reader/dramaturg, you can take the same liberties as the director of this production, and you may decide to be biased toward certain characters, but your duty is nonetheless that of understanding the dramatic conflict thoroughly so that you can develop an informed interpretation.

As you read the play, reflect on the potential impact of the dramatic conflict and try to ascertain the reasons sustaining characters' agendas and ideas. Instead of siding immediately with whom you perceive to be the most likable character, or what is the most acceptable idea, make a deliberate effort to consider other characters' points of view and probe how those views might be supported textually. Let your creativity run free as you envision the conflict and how it shapes every single aspect of the play.

Obstacles

Obstacles are impediments to the realization of a character's objectives. They represent what stands between the character and what she/he wants and can be internal (e.g., past traumas, psychological makeup) or external (e.g., people, objects, legal prescriptions, sociocultural customs). Understanding the obstacles and their ramifications is an important step in unpacking the nature of the conflict and the urgency of the action. It is also an invaluable tool for understanding the characters better. You can gain insight into the characters by how they decide to deal with the obstacle at hand: what strategies they use to overcome each obstruction. Do they tackle it directly? Do they resort to violence, or do they find a more sophisticated way to circumvent it? Do they give in? Do they persist despite failure?

Reflect on Hamlet's notorious reluctance to murder his uncle Claudius and see what kinds of obstacles he encounters that prevent him from performing the tragic deed. You will find that they vary vastly and include the presence of other characters in the scene, the king's guards, Hamlet's fear that Claudius might go to heaven, the gentle and intellectual nature of the protagonist, to name a few.

In their key roles as researchers and facilitators, dramaturgs understand that obstacles and conflicts provide a key for unlocking dramatic action and therefore must be investigated thoroughly. This exploration might lead to identifying the cultural significance of the characters' conflicts and obstacles, something that might help actors approach their roles with more subtlety and inform the director's viewpoint. The dramaturg's research might also aid the designers in their vision for the show by disclosing new visual perceptions and possible physical representations of conflict and obstacle.

Practicum

The following scene is from Sam Shepard's *True West* and portrays a confrontation between two brothers who want very different things. Try to identify each character's super-objective (the paramount objective that encompasses all others in the scene) and also each one's single objectives as represented in individual lines. Make sure you find active verbs to frame the characters' "wants."

AUSTIN: So you don't know how long you'll be staying, then?

LEE: Depends mostly on houses, ya' know.

AUSTIN: Houses?

LEE: Yeah. Houses. Electric devices. Stuff like that. I gotta' make a little tour first.

AUSTIN: Lee, why don't you just try another neighborhood, all right?

LEE: What'sa' matter with this neighborhood? This is a great neighborhood. Lush. Good class a' people. Not many dogs.

AUSTIN: Well, our uh—Our mother just happens to live here. That's all.

LEE: Nobody's gonna' know. All they know is somethin's missing. That's all. She'll never even hear about it. Nobody's gonna' know.

AUSTIN: You're going to get picked up if you start walking around here at night.

LEE: Me? I'm gonna' git picked up? What about you? You stick out like a sore thumb. Look at you. You think yer regular lookin'?

AUSTIN: I've got too much to deal with here to be worrying about—

LEE: Yer not gonna' have to worry about me! I've been doin' all right without you. I haven't been anywhere near you for five years! Now isn't that true?

AUSTIN: Yeah.

LEE: So you don't have to worry about me. I'm a free agent.

AUSTIN: All right.

LEE: Now all I wanna' do is borrow yer car.

AUSTIN: No!

LEE: Just fer a day. One day.

AUSTIN: No!

LEE:	I won't take it outside a twenty mile radius. I promise ya'. You can check the speedometer.
AUSTIN:	You're not borrowing my car! That's all there is to it.

(pause)

LEE:	Then I'll just take the damn thing.
AUSTIN:	Lee, look—I don't want any trouble, all right?
LEE:	That's a dumb line. That is a dumb fuckin' line. You git paid fer dreamin' up a line like that?
AUSTIN:	Look, I can give you some money if you need money.
LEE:	Don't you say that to me! Don't you ever say that to me! You may be able to git away with that with the Old Man. Git him tanked up for a week! Buy him off with yer Hollywood blood money, but not me! I can git my own money my own way. Big money!
AUSTIN:	I was just making an offer.
LEE:	Yeah, well keep it to yourself. (Shepard 8–9)

CHAPTER 3

Language

Language is the primary building block of a play and therefore one of the most relevant things dramaturgs tackle when they start researching a play. A play could hardly exist without language. Even the most avant-garde or modernist dramas usually need some linguistic content to exist as plays. Language is absolutely central because it relates directly to characterization, style, and genre; moreover, it allows us to make sense of what we read or experience in the theatre. Language does not simply communicate what characters want, it also tells us a whole lot about their personalities, and the forces that shaped their identities and their minds. By the same token, language reveals things of which characters might not be aware. It provides the audience with clues for understanding the wholeness of the character.

In approaching the language of a play there are several issues a dramaturg must consider carefully.

Grammar and Syntax

These two linguistic categories determine how we write and speak and codify how we express ourselves in communication with others. Syntax refers to how sentences are constructed, while grammar addresses the rules that regulate how one might use a given language correctly.

Train yourself to focus on how characters speak, and you will find you can understand easily who they are, what they believe in, and what they truly want. Does a character speak in short sentences or long? Does she/he ask a lot of questions? Is the speech educated and correct? Or is it low and ungrammatical? Those are queries that have the potential to open doors into the character's objectives and given circumstances. Take for instance the syntactical difference between active and passive sentences and reflect on how they express different degrees of agency and engagement with reality. Active sentences invite a more direct and powerful experience because they establish an immediate relationship between the agent and the receiver of the action. If I say "Hamlet stabs Polonius," I state a fact in which the subject (Hamlet) predicates his action on a transitive object (Polonius), and in so doing I do simplify the communication of the event by economizing on words and maintaining the directness and power of the action. If, on the other hand, I say that "Polonius was stabbed by Hamlet," I am far less direct in conveying the event because I position the object of the action at the beginning of the sentence and I turn the performer of the action of stabbing into an efficient cause. In this second iteration, the reader experiences the event in a filtered, oblique manner because the immediacy of the action is lost in the passive form, as is its violence.

Ponder also whether linguistic mistakes may be communicating aspects of the character that might not emerge through the dramatic action, or how they might embody the given circumstances of the character. Mistakes, whether grammatical or semantic, force readers and spectators to stop and think because they disrupt our expectation of order and harmony. They demand attention by asking us to focus on specific lexical items as well as on the speaker who utters them. For these reasons, they are never casual and must receive our full consideration. We laugh at Mrs. Malaprop's errors and mispronunciations in Richard Brinsley Sheridan's *The Rivals* because her misuse of words subverts linguistic conventions and forces us to place inappropriate terms in unsuitable contexts. In other plays, however, ungrammatical language shows and comments on the social circumstances of the characters. Reflect on the following dialogue from *Topdog/Underdog* where Booth confesses to his brother Lincoln that he murdered his girlfriend Grace:

BOOTH   Grace. I popped her. Grace
(*Rest*)

          Who thuh fuck she think she is doing me like she done? Telling me I dont got nothing going on. I showed her what I got going on. Popped her good. Twice. 3 times. Whatever.
(*Rest*)

          She aint dead.
(*Rest*)

          She weren't wearing my ring I gived her. Said it was too small. Fuck that. Said was into bigger things. Fuck that. Shes alive not to worry, she aint going out that easy, shes alive shes shes -.

LINCOLN: Dead. Shes –
BOOTH: Dead   (Roudané 681)

The grammatical mistakes in this dialogue are many: The third person pronouns ("he" and "she") do not carry the customary final "s" in the present tense, the simple past of "to give" is irregular, contractions are wrongly marked, words are misspelled, and sentences start with a verb and elide the subject altogether. The significance of grammatical mistakes in this passage goes way beyond the education of the speaker, Booth, who did not go to school, had a disadvantaged upbringing, and grew up without his parents. His utterances make more sense if we look at them within the context of hip hop culture because some of his speech patterns are reminiscent of the kind of street talk one hears in modern music. In this regard, what he says is both the result of a failing education and the adoption of a linguistic persona who has decided to speak in a way that defines him both culturally and racially. Moreover, his language must be contextualized within the specific moment of the play. In this scene, Booth has confessed to the murder of his girlfriend Grace and is just about to murder his own brother. His speech pattern and word choice highlight his anxious and panicky behavior and create a sense of uneasiness in the audience. Booth's language makes perfect sense once you frame it within the erratic and uncontrolled physical movements that you might expect from a person who is about to commit his second murder. The language fully delivers the contradictions of the character, his background, and his heartbreaking destiny.

Syntax, or sentence construction, may reveal a lot about characters' education, class, age, gender, geographical origin, ethnicity, and other characteristics. Syntax can, in brief, contribute to our understanding of the given circumstances.

Lexicon

The choice of words that characters use to express themselves is revealing of their background and outlook on life. Does the character use rich and flowery adjectives, or opt for a minimalistic and efficient way of communication? How can characters' lexicon translate their given circumstances? When reading a play, make sure you pay special attention to how words are selected and the function they serve within the dialogue. Always question why one word was chosen over another and the precise purpose words have in describing specific characters or situations. Do this especially with words that sound unusual, surprising, or old-fashioned to your ears, as they might hold crucial significance for the plot and the characterization. In Harold Pinter's *Old Times*, for instance,

Anna employs the old-fashioned word "lest" in her conversation with Deeley:

> ANNA: No one who lived here would want to go far. I would not want to go far, I would be afraid of going far, lest when I returned the house would be gone.
> DEELEY: Lest?
> ANNA: What?
> DEELEY: The word lest. Haven't heard it in a long time (19)

The dissonance created by "lest" is central to the dramaturgy of the play because this could be the moment in which Deeley realizes he heard the word many years ago, and from Anna herself, when they all lived in London. It is also a focal word due to its meaning, which implies caution or fear of some sort of danger. In fact, as a word, lest describes perfectly the atmosphere of ambiguity and potential violence that permeates the play and aptly epitomizes the "comedy of menace" with which Pinter is usually associated.

Figures of Speech

The English word *trope* refers to all figures of speech and describes the action of "turning" and a sense of change and manipulation. Trope encompasses various figures of speech such as metaphor, simile, and synecdoche, where a comparison is established between objects that might, or might not, share similarities. In this regard, a trope states an identity between two objects while simultaneously stressing their independence from each other. Metaphors, for instance, enlarge possible significations and expand the potential of a word or an image by opening up further interpretations. If I describe someone's eyes as "shining stars," I am clearly using an overused and simple metaphor, but I am also amplifying meaning by creating further frames to understand the nature and significance of those eyes to me. For instance, they might bright my life, guide me when I am in the dark, or allow me to see my world more clearly. Figures of speech have the capacity to clarify reality by providing the reader/spectator with multiple interpretive frames. Due to their malleable and multifunctional properties, they provide us with fresh readings of the play. Finally, figures of speech are not only instrumental in elucidating deeper meaning within the play text, they also shed light on possible images for its staging.

Subtext

If the dialogue occurring between characters is the text, what goes unsaid between them is the subtext. The subtext of a character is what she/he cannot, or does not want to, say due to reasons that may be clarified by the story. This is a strategy that puts the readers/spectators in the privileged position of knowing more than the characters and that fosters a sense of expectation for what is to come. As a tool for sophisticated characterization, the subtext problematizes the representation of a given character by showing that she/he might have multiple objectives and also adds nuance to the story.

In the following scene from David Rabe's *Hurlyburly*, Darlene has just confessed to Eddie that she had had an abortion years before and that, since she was seeing two men at the same time, she did not know who the father of the baby was. Eddie is quite shocked at the news but does not want to show his emotions for fear of seeming narrow-minded or jealous. However, his disbelief that Darlene could go out with two guys at the same time and feel the same about both of them emerges in the subtext:

DARLENE: Okay. It's just something I'm very, sometimes, sensitive about.

EDDIE: Sure. What? The abortion?

DARLENE: Yeah.

EDDIE: Sure. Okay, though? You okay now? You feel okay?

DARLENE: I'm hungry. You hungry? (*Goes to the kitchen to look for something to nibble on*)

EDDIE: I mean, if we don't talk these things out, we'll just end up with all this, you know, unspoken shit, following us around. You wanna go out and eat? Let's go out. What are you hungry for? How about Chinese?

DARLENE: Sure.

EDDIE: (*Grabbing up the phone and starting to dial*) We could go to Mr. Chou's. Treat ourselves right.

DARLENE: That's great. I love the seaweed.

EDDIE: I mean, you want Chinese?

DARLENE: I love Mr. Chou's.

EDDIE: We could go some other place. How about Ma Maison?

DARLENE: Sure.

EDDIE:	(*Hanging up the phone*). You like that better than Mr. Chou's?
DARLENE:	It doesn't matter to me.
EDDIE:	Which one should I call?
DARLENE:	Surprise me.
EDDIE:	I don't want to surprise you. I want to, you know, do whatever you really want.
DARLENE:	Then just pick one. Call one. Either.
EDDIE:	I mean, why should I have to guess? I don't want to guess. Just tell me. I mean, what if I pick the wrong one?
DARLENE:	You can't pick the wrong one. Honestly, Eddie, I like them both the same. I like them both exactly the same.
EDDIE:	Exactly?
DARLENE:	Yes, I like them both.
EDDIE:	I mean how can you possibly think you like them both the same? One is French and one is Chinese. They're different. They're as different as—Darlene, the only thing they have in common is that THEY'RE BOTH RESTAURANTS!
DARLENE:	Are you aware that you're yelling?
EDDIE:	My voice is raised for emphasis! (Rabe 326–328)

Choosing a restaurant is not the issue here, it is merely a strategy for Eddie to question Darlene's feelings about the two guys and a way to channel his frustration in an indirect way. If the text spoken by the characters is the tip of the iceberg visible above the water, the subtext is what lies beneath the surface. As a reader/dramaturg, you want to make sure you understand the subtext really well otherwise you could miss entirely the characterization and the overall meaning of the play.

Language and the Sense of Place/Space

I would like to start this section with the definitions of *place* and *space* that Michel de Certeau gives in his landmark book *The Practice of Everyday Life*, because I believe that they frame effectively our discussion of how language shapes theatrical places and spaces.

A place (*lieu*) is the order (of whatever kind) in accord with which elements are distributed in relationship of coexistence. It thus excludes the possibility of two things being in the same location (*place*). The law of the "proper" rules in the place: the elements taken into consideration are beside one another, each situated in its own "proper" and distinct location, a location it defines. A place is thus an instantaneous configuration of positions. It implies an indication of stability.

A *space* exists when one takes into consideration vectors of direction, velocities and time variables. Thus space is composed of intersections of mobile elements. It is in a sense actuated by the ensemble of movements deployed within it. Space occurs as the effect produced by the operations that orient it, situate it, temporalize it, and make it function in a polyvalent unity of conflictual programs or contractual proximities. On this view, in relation to place, space is like the word when it is spoken, that is, when it is caught in the ambiguity of an actualization, transformed into a term dependent upon many different conventions, situated as the act of a present (or of a time), and modified by the transformations caused by successive contexts. In contradistinction to the place, it has thus none of the univocity or stability of a "proper." In short, *space is a practiced place*. (117)

As an example, reflect on the setting of Act II of William Shakespeare's *Othello*, Cyprus. If you think of Cyprus as an island in the Mediterranean that is under the protection of Venice and has come under threat of Turkish attack, then you would think of Cyprus as a "place," according to de Certeau's interpretation. On the other hand, if you imagine Cyprus as an inescapable tiny piece of land surrounded by the sea and inhabited by plotting and evil characters where social perception is everything, you start envisioning a "space," one that is "practiced," following de Certeau, because it is situated within a dynamic setting and conflicting characters' agendas.

In studying a play you confront both place and space, which means that you have to understand the significance of specific geographical sites (e.g., cities, regions, nations) and physical locales (e.g., buildings, rooms) both in their literal and symbolical interpretations. This is a meaningful exercise because eventually you want to figure out how the place and space described in the play might be reconfigured within the theatre. As you know, theatre can create a sense of space through sets, lighting, props, costumes, music, movement, and media. The theatrical contract implies that as audience members we will believe the world of the play as long as it makes sense within the dramatic coordinates written by the playwright and interpreted by the director and the creative team. To a seventeenth-century spectator, taking a few steps might have meant travelling to the opposite side of the globe, and a slight turn of the head meant the character could address the audience directly, as if in a very private place, without being heard by others. Theatrical conventions of all times, even the ones more rooted in realism and naturalism, allowed for theatre to articulate diverse and sometimes jarring spaces. When characters claim to be somewhere, anywhere, readers and/or spectators actively construct a mental image that accounts for what they might know about that specific locale (place) and how that locale is represented on the stage and is brought to life by the design elements and the performers (space).

The sense of place/space, which is the communication of the spatial reality of the play, is often shaped by language. Words, sentences, and dialogue can conjure up places, and as a reader/dramaturg, you must attune your eyes and ears to the sense of location the playwright conveys in order to fully comprehend the nuances of the text and possible clues about how to stage the play. In the case of older dramas, characters might simply comment on the setting of the story by stating the city, the room in the house in which the scene takes place, and so on. In other cases, however, it is up to the attentive reader/dramaturg to detect shifts in place because that information might be couched in the nuances of the language. Take, for example, the last monologue of *The Glass Menagerie*, where Tom describes what happened to him after he left Amanda and Laura, respectively his mother and sister, in their St. Louis apartment while he took off to travel the world. The previous scene ended with Tom having a dramatic fight with Amanda and his final departure. Tom is now addressing the audience from the fire-escape landing, which throughout the play represents Tom's desire for emancipation and freedom. There are several indicators that the place of the scene is shifting and moving from the "here" of the monologue, the fire escape, to other locales Tom visited during his wanderings.

> I didn't go to the moon, I went much further—for time is the longest distance between two places—Not long after that I was fired for writing a poem on the lid of a shoe-box.

I left Saint Louis. I descended the steps of this fire-escape for a last time and followed, from then on, in my father's footsteps, attempting to find in motion what was lost in space—I traveled around a great deal. The cities swept about me like dead leaves, leaves that were brightly colored but torn away from the branches. I would have stopped, but I was pursued by something. It always came upon me unawares, taking me altogether by surprise. Perhaps it was a familiar bit of music. Perhaps it was only a piece of transparent glass—perhaps I am walking along a street at night, in some strange city, before I have found companions. I pass the lighted window of a shop where perfume is sold. The window is filled with pieces of colored glass, tiny transparent bottles in delicate colors, like bits of shattered rainbow. Then all at once my sister touches my shoulder. I turn around and look into her eyes . . . Oh, Laura, Laura, I tried to leave you behind me, but I am more faithful than I intended to be! I reach for a cigarette, I cross the street, I run into the movies or a bar, I buy a drink, I speak to the nearest stranger—anything that can blow your candles out! (*Laura bends over the candles.*)—for nowadays the world is lit by lightning! Blow your candles, Laura—and so good-bye . . . (*She blows the candles out.*) (339–340)

Tom's urge to find "in motion what was lost in space" is an important indicator to decipher the scene's sense of place, which is marked by the whirlwind of Tom's travelling from place to place. The major shift in place/space happens in the middle of the monologue with the transition from the past tense to the present, "Perhaps I am walking. . .". Tom stops narrating past events and places himself in the present of his own memories, and as readers we perceive that shift as powerful because the dramatic stakes become higher and more pressing. There is a merging of time(s) and place(s) in this scene as we see Tom literally regressing into his past to situate himself firmly within his memories, so firmly, in fact, that he is using the present to communicate the tangible immediacy of the moment. This scene is palimpsestic in that as readers and spectators we are allowed to see the simultaneous emergence of different realities: We experience the resilience of the past in the present, and the manifestation of such resilience in the collapsing of the "here" of the performance to the "there" of the past narrative. We are also invited to follow Tom in his vagabond life and experience snippets of his travelling from place to place. The fact that during Tom's monologue Laura is visible on stage, and is about to blow out the candles, makes this sense of place/space and time quite extraordinary.

Dialects and Accents

A dialect is a linguistic variation that occurs within the same language: there are American dialects, British dialects, Australian dialects, and many others. The language is the same, but the way it is spoken can be dramatically different. An accent, instead, describes the linguistic utterances of someone who speaks a language other than her/his own: for instance, an Italian person speaking English with an Italian accent. Playwrights might or might not notate in their text a character's dialect or accent, but as a dramaturg/reader, you should conjure a sense of sound when you mentally hear the text spoken by the various characters, especially if the play is set in a geographical location that is different from the one where you are or one that you come from. You should not worry about pinpointing the specific soundscape of the play because only trained dialect coaches can really capture the nuances of dialects and accents and reproduce them authentically. What matters most is that you are aware that characters do not necessarily share your own cultural and linguistic world. They are different from you! They speak differently, and they act differently. One must locate them in their cultural circumstances, and try to understand them in their own specificities. Reading *Steel Magnolias*, a play by Robert Harling set in Louisiana, would be a much richer experience if one hears it through a Southern drawl. Moreover, it would be a lot more entertaining if you attune yourself to hear mentally a different dialect because you might find its "strangeness" enticing and captivating.

Dialects are invaluable markers of class, status, and education, as demonstrated in George Bernard Shaw's plays, for instance. They can also establish differences and ranks, as shown by Eugene O'Neill's *Moon of the Caribbees*, *In the Zone*, and *Bound East for Cardiff*, three plays set at sea where the reader experiences many dialects and accents at once.

Silences and Pauses

I have illustrated so far the role language plays in the reader/dramaturg's interpretation of the play, but there is more to a play than words and sentences. If one has to do justice to a dramatic text and make an intelligent hypothesis about how it might be staged, it is essential to account for how silences and pauses are scripted by the playwright and interpreted by the director and actors during the performance.

A pause is short gap of time between lines, or between words within a line, often used for dramatic effect, as one character searches for the right word or takes in the response of the person to whom she/he is talking. A silence is a longer pause and can illustrate a character at a loss for words, but also a shift in dramatic focus, for instance due to a change in conversational topics or a jump in the temporal frame of the story. While it has become unusual to find indications of silences and pauses in the stage directions of modern plays, there are playwrights who use both abundantly. British Nobel Prize winner Harold Pinter is notorious for interspersing his dialogue with pauses and silences that contribute to creating a menacing effect and confound the expectations of readers and spectators alike. Consider the very beginning of *Old Times*, one of his most famous plays, and reflect on how what is not said amplifies the capacity for dramatic effect.

Lights dim. Three figures discerned.
DEELEY slumped in armchair, still.
KATE curled on a sofa, still.
ANNA standing at the window, looking out.

Silence

Lights up on DEELEY and KATE, smoking cigarettes.

ANNA's figure remains still in dim light at the window.

KATE: (*Reflectively*) Dark.

Pause

DEELEY: Fat or thin?
KATE: Fuller than me, I think.

Pause

DEELEY: She was then?
KATE: I think so.
DEELEY: She may not be now.

Pause

                    Was she your best friend?
KATE: Oh, what does that mean?

DEELEY:	What?
KATE:	The word friend . . . when you look back . . . all that time.
DEELEY:	Can you remember what you felt?

Pause

KATE:	It is a very long time. (7–8)

The silence at the beginning of the play allows for the geography of the space and the physical relationship of the characters to resonate with the readers/spectators. Just as dialogue does not always reveal, so silence does not always hide. In this specific case, the silence is quite ripe with possibilities. We take in where the characters sit or stand and the position of their bodies, we wonder what they are thinking and make hypotheses about what they will do next, and we construct an inner life for the characters. At the top of the scene, it makes sense that the silence is chosen over the shorter pause, because the central image of the three characters is quite pregnant with meaning and sets up the tone of the piece. On the other hand, the pauses allow for Deeley's and Kate's lines to fill the time between the present of the question ("Fat or thin?") to the uncertain past of the answer ("Fuller than me, I think"). Dramaturgically, the pause suggests that one is still within the same conversation, but that the conversation is far from being realistic. At the end of Act I, silences indicate a temporal shift to the past where characters are seemingly transported to their youth and relive some mysterious trauma that impacted them all.

In the cases of pauses and silences, the reader/dramaturg must consider how the absence of words is significant in the dramaturgical context. What actions appear evident? Who holds the power? What kind of struggle or conflict is the playwright highlighting? What possibilities do silences and pauses open up for the staging of the play? Are they merely the absence of dialogue, or are they instead filling that absence with questions, symbols, and metaphors to be deciphered? More importantly, what kind of responsibility do they give to the reader/spectator?

Regardless of whether the play you are reading marks silences and pauses, make all efforts to "hear" the text and reflect on how the lines might be delivered with gaps of various lengths between them. Once you determine the objectives of the character, explore how silences and pauses might enhance them.

Genre

Language helps the reader/dramaturg identify the world of the characters; therefore, it is useful to consider genre expectations as guiding principles to make sense of the play as a whole. Knowing that we are dealing with a comedy, rather than a tragedy or a farce, can immediately tune us into relevant sociocultural viewpoints. Mistaking the genre of a play that you are either reading or dramaturging can have unexpected and unfortunate consequences!

Tragedy

The genre of tragedy, which Aristotle placed at the pinnacle of all literary endeavors, is possibly one of the most studied by academics and loved by audiences worldwide. There are many denominations of tragedy that illustrate dramaturgical variances, periodization issues, and geographical differences: classical tragedy, Elizabethan tragedy, heroic tragedy, domestic tragedy, and many others. However, they all share, to some extent, the following characteristics:

- Classical tragedy often deals with aristocratic or upper class characters who are placed within inescapable situations in which they have to make decisions that will thoroughly impact their reality. With the emergence of the middle class as the new driving political, economic, and social force, tragedy has incorporated characters of all social classes.
- Tragedy represents a moment of profound crisis in which the order of the play's world has been compromised. The tragic hero is caught between a rock and a hard place. She/he will have to act, and the decision taken will bring about her/his demise.
- The hero experiences *hamartia*, a word that should not be confused with *hubris* (arrogance or pride), as it is sometimes understood in theatre classes. *Hamartia* points in the direction of a missing of the mark, a mistake in evaluating one's own circumstances and the failure to realize the unfolding of one's own destiny. In this sense, the character's *hamartia* often carries the moral responsibility for having damaged the very people (family members, friends, and fellow citizens) that the hero wanted to protect in the first place. This brings about a profound sense of shame that might lead to the climax of the play with its tragic consequences.

- The hero experiences a reversal of fortune, or *peripeteia* (from good to bad, or from bad to worse).
- The hero experiences recognition when a part of her/his past, possibly a secret, is revealed. This is what the Greeks called *anagnorisis*, an episode that will bring about an awareness that the hero did not have before. This knowledge is often profoundly connected with her/his downfall and might happen at the same time as her/his demise.
- Reversal and recognition might be envisioned as intersecting trajectories that by meeting produce maximum knowledge and minimum social status. This is certainly true for Oedipus in *Oedipus the King*, where the hero knows everything about his past, the very moment he finds himself destitute and exiled.
- *Anagnorisis* is often connected to miasma, a state of contamination or pollution that can be both moral and physical. Miasma can lead to expulsion or barring from the collectivity because it has the potential to spread in literal or symbolical ways. At the very end of *Oedipus the King*, the protagonist willingly chooses self-exile because he knows his current status of impurity is unsuitable for social living.
- The dramatic stakes of tragedy are high. Characters might be in danger, and death is always a possibility, even when it does not occur.
- It might employ a poetic, magniloquent, and solemn language that suits the characters and their predicaments.
- According to Aristotle, tragedy brings about feelings of pity and fear. Pity for the predicaments of the characters who may have not deserved what happened to them; fear that those situations might be revisited on us or on people we love.
- The highest point of dramatic tension is called catharsis. There might be more than one catharsis in a tragedy.

Comedy

The world of comedy is surprisingly similar to that of tragedy. One could argue that is not the topics or the themes that differentiate the two genres, but rather how these topics and themes are dealt with in the play through plot, characterization, and the world outlook adopted by the playwright. Comedy focuses on the inexhaustible resilience of the characters who fight back in the face of impending disaster because they are animated by an undying faith in life. On the other hand, tragic characters must succumb to their destiny. The dramatic trajectory of comedy is toward the continuation of life, whereas that of tragedy exhausts itself in the characters' total consummation. There are some basic notions and ideas that can help up identify comedy and distinguish it from other genres. These are a few of them:

- The world of comedy is rife with plots that might draw on conjugal problems; conflicts between parents and children; unrequited love between characters of different ages and social classes; and misconceptions, misguided assumptions, disguises, and practical jokes. The world of comedy is domestic in that it is often set within a household or a family.
- Comedic characters are resilient. They never give up on life, instead they are eager to live it fully and pleasurably.
- In the world of comedy, there are lower linguistic standards and more colloquial and idiomatic tones.
- Comedic characters are often members of the lower classes. They often display more common sense and intelligence than the wealthy people for whom they work.
- Their speech can be crass, drawing on vulgar topics such as sexual exploits, petty crimes, inextinguishable hunger, and bodily functions.
- Comedy strongly emphasizes change and transformation, especially with lower-class characters trying to get the upper hand on their superiors. However, it rarely translates this desire for change into a fully realized upward mobility as characters tend to remain in their own class. It upsets the order of society, but in the end reconfirms the old status quo. The difference is that the readers are aware of the moral superiority of the lower-class and downtrodden characters.
- *Bathos,* which can be loosely translated as the "feeling of the contrary," is an intrinsic strategy of comedy that plays with upsetting conventional and socially expected behaviors. Think about Tartuffe from the homonymous Moliere play and how surprising it is for the reader to find out he is a conniving thief and a womanizer dressed in the clothes of a religious man.
- Like tragedy, comedy presents itself in different forms varying from comedy of manners to *commedia dell'arte,* from classical

comedy to high comedy and farce; or, even more specifically, from Aristophanes' Greek Old Comedy to Menander's New Comedy.

Tragicomedy

This genre stages tragic stories but with happy endings, and its setting is usually pastoral and idyllic with characters who are shepherds, farmers, nymphs, and satyrs. While the existence of tragicomedy has been debated since classical times, with Aristotle arguing that tragedies did not have to end in death, and with Plautus, in ancient Rome, arguing that a play did not have to be either a tragedy or a comedy, the dramaturgical formalization of tragicomedy happened during the Renaissance in Italy. It was with the translation of Aristotle's *Poetics* that Italian dramatists and theoreticians started to question what genre was better suited to their time, and elaborated new genres altogether. The first successful examples of tragicomedy are *Pastor Fido* by G.B. Guarini and *Aminta* by Torquato Tasso. Their language, characters, and plots are similar to those of tragedy, but where tragedy would escalate to a climax through the completion of the tragic deed, tragicomedy resolves all conflicts and ends happily. Consider the basic plot of *Aminta*, a play that had an enormous impact in shaping the direction of European theatre in the sixteenth and seventeenth centuries and was so popular it was adapted into ballets and operas: the hero, Aminta, is a shepherd who is in love with Silvia, a beautiful nymph who has dedicated her life to the goddess Diana and prefers hunting in the wilderness to falling in love. One day Silvia is attacked by a satyr and Aminta saves her, but she runs away from him nonetheless. The hero is so desperate that he walks off a cliff and everybody believes he is dead. At this point Silvia feels remorseful for having ignored him and realizes her true feeling for the forlorn youth. She goes to the site of the accident to cry over his body, but the hero, who has not hurt himself seriously, revives and the two are finally reunited as lovers.

Farce

Farce takes to the extreme some of the characteristics of comedy. Its plots are usually very intricate with many twists and turns and situations that might push the limits of believability. A farce normally stages many coincidences, misunderstandings, and absurd occurrences that audiences might find improbable in a more serious play, but that they are willing to accept given the conventions of the genre. Farcical characters can be over the top and affected in how they represent human nature's foibles or unusual behaviors. While considered a light form of entertainment, farces can also pack a punch when they explore notions of justice, social status, and gender relationship, to mention just a few of farce's favorite topics. George Feydeau perfected the farce in nineteenth-century France, but this genre has been around for a long time and it is still widely popular today. David Hirson's *La Bête*, for instance, was a huge success in its London West End run and it is still a favorite of college theatres in North America for its vibrant characters, hilarious situations, and fast pace.

Satire

While a farce will always provoke some sort of humorous reaction (if not a laugh, at least a giggle or a chuckle), satire may or may not be comical. Satirical plays expose and ridicule vices, excesses, and behaviors the playwright deems dangerous, unacceptable, or ludicrous. Using dramaturgical techniques grounded in parody, sarcasm, irony, and caricature, the satire pokes fun at social customs and acts as a biting social commentary that can vary from funny reproach to abrasive critique. Dario Fo, Italian playwright and Nobel laureate, is famous for his satirical portrayal of political and religious figures. In his landmark play *Mistero Buffo*, he lampoons Pope Boniface VIII (1235–1303), who was famous for his predilection for luxurious clothes, his liberal sexual mores, and his gruesome acts such as that of having people nailed by their tongue for having spoken against him or the ruling class. Consider the following exchange between the pope and a clumsy choirboy who helped him get dressed and is now accompanying him in a religious procession:

> (*He stops immediately and makes the gesture of yanking on the coat. He is holding himself back, exhausted and furious*).
> Who has their foot on my cloak? . . . (*He looks over his shoulder in a rage*) Tone deaf! Get off it! You can't sing! You're tone deaf! You don't lift up the cloak, and you put your feet on it . . . Watch out! . . . I've got my eye on

you! . . . I'll nail you to the main door by your tongue!
Tongue, nail, door, hammer – TON TON TON!
(*He quickly mimes the action of the nailing, then proceeds
to draw in the air an image of the choirboy nailed by his
tongue swaying in the wind as he hangs. He lets out a groan
that sounds like the door squeaking on its hinges*). (Fo 165)

This amusing moment, which is repeated several times with
slight variation throughout the scene, satirizes the pope's conduct
on the grounds that it is diametrically opposite to what would
be expected of the leader of the Christian world. Its buoyancy is
undercut by the mordant criticism of the medieval Catholic Church,
which, in the mind of the readers/spectators, inevitably leads to
more modern criticisms of the religious institution.

Style

The style of a play refers to its mode of linguistic and aesthetic
expression. Style is a term that relates both to the personal style a
playwright might have, as well as to the style of the period in which
she/he writes. For instance, it can point to the personal style of Jean
Racine's *Phedra*, as different from that of his contemporary Pierre
Corneille's *The Cid*, but also to the neoclassical style of the seventeenth century. Moreover, it always describes how a play presents
itself to its readership or audience. For instance, the style of a play
can be innovative or old, formal or colloquial, high or low; it can
also be, for example, realistic, metatheatrical, episodic, anti-realistic.
These are characteristics that are always perceived within the context
of the play's dramaturgy, as well as the audience's reception of it.

Style also illustrates the specific genre of a play, because we
normally comment on tragic or comic style. Let us now illustrate
some elements of style and discuss how they enhance the readers/
audience's experience.

Exposition

The reader/spectator must be in the position to make sense of the
story that the play portrays. The information she/he needs is conveyed through the plot, that is, through the way the story is constructed in the given play. Exposition relates to the description of
dramatic actions that have happened either before the play started
or offstage. In older plays, exposition normally occurs at the beginning of the play to act as a framework for the action that is to come.

Sometimes the revelation of the background of the story is delayed to generate anticipation and to heighten the expectations of the audience. Pieces of the past might be communicated at different climactic moments. This type of exposition allows for a co-construction of the story in which the reader/spectator is more engaged in unlocking and deconstructing the reality of the characters. It is more common in modern plays that have been strongly impacted by the birth of psychology.

Narrator

As a dramaturgical device, the narrator allows the spectators to have a personal interlocutor within the play. As if in a private conversation, or in a sort of confessional setting, the narrator will provide context for specific scenes, relay episodes from the past, comment on the present state of affairs, and speculate about what future actions might bring. Since the narrator breaks the fourth wall to address the audience directly, she/he is found more often in non-realistic plays. One of the most well-known examples is the narrator in Thornton Wilder's *Our Town* who guides the reader/ spectator through the story, introduces the numerous characters, and provides context for the play's events.

Representational Style

In this mode of expression, the audience is invited to sit back and enjoy the ride provided by reading the play or watching it in the theatre. The reality of the stage and that of the audience are completely separate. This style is the one more associated with realism or naturalism, where the circumstances presented on stage are made to look and feel as if they might happen in real life.

Metatheatrical Style

As suggested by the prefix "meta," which refers to an experience or an object that goes beyond its own reality, that moves and changes past its original state, metatheatrical style implies that the both the dramaturgy of the play and physical space of the theatre are permeable and subject to re-contextualization. It includes the "play-within-a-play" form, where the medium turns its critical means on itself and self-reflectively comments on its representational paradigms, such as actors breaking out of character, or more simply any strategy that destabilizes the convention of the representation. In this style, the audience is more active in figuring out both characters and story, and it may be addressed by the actors (in this case spectators are merely silent partners in a unidirectional conversation) or become almost another character (co-participation in the performance). This style is more common in non-realistic plays. Think of Greek comedy and how it often portrays real people who were known to the audience and thus plays with the fictional nature of the medium. Or consider the convention of the prologue in Renaissance comedy, where an actor addresses the spectators directly asking them to be kind toward the playwright and explaining briefly what the play is about.

Episodic Style

The narration is segmented and does not necessarily follow a chronology. The audience is asked to fill the temporal gaps between episodes and imagine what might have happened in between scenes. This style was made popular by Bertolt Brecht's Epic Theatre in plays such as *Mother Courage and Her Children* and *Galileo*, where the fragmentation of the narrative served to thwart climax and invite critical reflection and problem solving about the social issues portrayed on stage.

Mood and Tone

The mood of a play, also commonly referred to as its atmosphere, is the play's overall emotional quality. It is conveyed by imagery, language, and characterization in the written text and delivered onto the stage by director, designers, and actors through the *mise en scène*. It is also immediately reflected in the feelings that the play, both as text and as performance, elicits in readers and spectators alike. It has to do with the kind of emotional dispositions it generates, as well as the long-lasting impressions it evokes. While the characters' moods can change due to shifting circumstances and actions, the mood of the play is consistent, easily identifiable, and illustrative of the play as a whole. The mood can be dark or happy, somber or comical, tragic or farcical; in brief, it defines concisely, often with just a few adjectives, the type of world the characters inhabit.

The mood of Stephen Dietz's theatrical adaptation of Bram Stoker's *Dracula*, for example, is quite evident from the very beginning of the piece: It draws on macabre imagery and mysterious characters; it depends on special effects to create sudden appearances and disappearances; it exploits fog machines and shadowy environments to enhance the sense of terror; and ultimately it looks at a bygone world of legendary tales as both exotic and sentimental. Nobody would ever mistake the mood of Dietz's *Dracula* with that of a classical tragedy that might also be dealing with death and horrible events, but does so through somber and solemn feelings. This distinction becomes even more obvious if you experience *Dracula* in the theatre and find yourself waiting with trepidation the frightful appearance of the protagonist.

As you read a play and come to determine its general mood, know that mood by itself cannot provide you with a full understanding of the play unless it is situated in a rigorous study of characters and dramatic action. Mood is descriptive and generic, your analysis of the play must be instead focused, objective, and critical.

Mood is sometimes confused with tone, while in reality the two are quite different. While mood can be defined as the spirit of the play and has to do with the organic feelings and emotions that the play brings out in the reader/spectator, tone has to do with how the playwright conveys her/his ideas to you. It describes the quality of the playwright's voice, as narrator of the story, and it is intrinsically tied to how she/he has crafted and emplotted the story, the kind of syntax she/he used, and the sort of relationship she/he aspires to create with her/his readership and spectatorship. Analyzing the language is the first step to understand the tone of a play because it allows you to come closer to how the playwright really feels about the characters and their circumstances. Is the playwright patronizing the characters? Is she/he judging or sentimentalizing their predicaments? How does the playwright couch her/his voice in the play? Does she/he have stand-ins among the characters who speak for her/him? Determining all these factors can give you a good idea of the tone of the play.

Translation

When dealing with translated plays, you want to try to read as many versions as possible. Different translations reflect different views of the world of the play and its characters, and as such they give varied interpretations of the story. It is through the reading of diverse translations that you might be able to understand what the playwright really meant when she/he wrote the play. This is particularly true if you do not speak the original language of the play and must rely entirely on translations. Even old translations that might sound awkward due to obsolete word choices and syntax can provide you with essential information about the play and clarify doubts you might have about word meaning and textual nuances. A brief example from Federico García Lorca's *Blood Wedding* can shed light on the importance of consulting multiple translations of the play you are reading. The stage directions in Act One specify that the Bride lives in a *cueva*, a cave, a location we usually associate with primitive dwellings and certainly not with the life style of a young woman whose father is described as being a wealthy landowner. If you read the translation by Ted Hughes, you would miss the reference to the cave completely since he translates the Spanish term as "house." However, if you consult the translations by Gwynne Edwards and Peter Luke, and the recent one by Caridad Svitch, you find out they translated *cueva* correctly as cave because in Andalusia, where the play is set, it is still quite common to have houses built in the rocky hillside of mountains, and those residences look like caves because they are literally caves, no matter the domestic comforts they may offer. The fact that the Bride lives in one of those caves shows that she is located further into the country (in the play the trip to get to her place is described as long and arduous), but the cave, as a rustic dwelling, also serves to frame her wild and indomitable nature, the one she will display in the final act by running away with Leonardo on the day she is supposed to wed the Groom. By translating *cueva* as house, one loses both social and textual references and thus runs the risk of doing a superficial reading of the play. As a second example, consider the lines spoken by the Mother when she realizes that the Bride has escaped and left her son at the altar. Here is the translation by Gwynne Edwards and Peter Luke:

FATHER:	It can't be her. Perhaps she's thrown herself into the water-tank.
MOTHER:	Only decent and clean girls throw themselves into the water. Not that one! But now she's my son's wife. Two sides. Now there are two sides here. (*They all enter.*) My family and yours. All of you must go. Shake the dust from your shoes. Let's go and help my son. (*The people split into two groups.*) He's got plenty of family: his cousins from the coast and all those from inland. Go out from here! Search all the

roads. The hour of blood has come again. Two sides. You on yours, me on mine. After them! Get after them! (73)

This translation was first published in England in 1987 and shows its age. While it is quite faithful to the original, it is also too literal and rigid to be spoken comfortably by actors on stage. Not only does it use odd words ("water-tank" instead of the more direct "well"), it also lacks fluidity. The fact that the syntax is choppy and seems to slow down the Mother's speech is almost counterintuitive to the sense of urgency the scene wants to communicate. After all she wants everybody to get ready immediately to pursue the man who ran away with her son's bride! Consider now the 2009 translation by Caridad Svitch, a prolific Latina playwright and translator who has been working as a practicing theatre artist for a long time.

FATHER OF THE BRIDE: It can't be her. Maybe she threw herself into the well.

THE MOTHER: Honorable girls, pure girls, throw themselves into the river. But not this one! Yet she's my son's wife now, so . . . Two groups. We have two groups, here. [*All enter*] My family and yours. Everyone sets out from here. Dust off your shoes, and let's help my son. [*They separate into two groups*] He has his family: his cousins from the coast and all the others. Away then! Search for them everywhere! The hour of blood has come again. Two groups. You with yours and I with mine. After them! After them! (180)

Here we are dealing with a more agile translation that takes into account a few essential facts: These lines will be heard from the mouths of actors so they must sound believable; the words must convey the urgency of the moment and the dramatic drive of the scene; the Mother brings to the table the issue of honor when she discusses what a honorable girl would have done, and this is essential because the code of behavior of Lorca's characters is steeped in notions of honor; and, finally, in Svitch's translation literalness is less important than performability.

Postdramatic Theatre

At this point it is worth addressing briefly the emergence of a new category of plays that have been named postdramatic after the title of Hans-Theis Lehmann's book, *Postdramatic Theatre*, which was originally published in German in 1999. The author describes mainly plays written after the 1960s that shy away from the rigidity of Aristotelian dramaturgy and its reliance on text. Lehmann argues that postdramatic theatre moves past the preeminence of the verbal text and focuses instead on the performer's body and space as dominant coordinates of the theatrical event. Postdramatic theatre places the spectators in an active role in shaping and making sense of the performance and charges them with the responsibility of making up their own minds. This means that the text does not force the audience into experiencing a unifying vision of the story, but rather presents them with interweaving and ambiguous narratives that might not speak to each other directly. You can see how this style inherently undermines the representational paradigms of dramatic theatre where the story follows a narrative arc that places conflict and catharsis as priorities, and where the audience members are normally in the position of observers. Some of the artists and theatre groups commonly associated with the postdramatic are the Wooster Group, Robert Lepage, Robert Wilson, Heiner Müller, Romeo Castellucci, and many others. While Lehmann's notion of the postdramatic is not totally new to theatre, his book jumpstarted new theoretical discourses about representation and it created critical waves that are still deeply felt in the field of Theatre and Performance Studies.

The question we must ask at this point is how we, as reader/dramaturgs, should approach a postdramatic play? Each work will demand to be treated in specific ways, so it is hard to address standard practices to read postdramatic plays consistently. Nevertheless, there are some stylistic and aesthetic qualities that you may consider and that can provide you with some general guidelines:

- Since the postdramatic places little emphasis on linguistic text, you have to rely on video of theatrical productions, director's notes, design sketches, dramaturgical program notes, pictures, and any other source of information available to fully appreciate a postdramatic event. The text will not help you much, by itself, in understanding the totality of the theatrical event and it might be very brief and difficult to comprehend.

- Many postdramatic plays draw on previous original works and can be better understood through the lens of adaptation. These works might be using well-known plays to comment on their themes and characters and argue in favor or against their ideas, or they might simply use the original source as a narrative frame to address completely different topics. You will have to make decisions about dramaturgical objectives of the postdramatic piece after careful consideration of both original source and adaptation. For instance, if you are dealing with *Hamletmachine* by Heiner Müller, you want to make sure that you understand the Shakespearean *Hamlet* in its original incarnation before you move to unpack the adapted text in its postdramatic vision. Once you have done the necessary research on *Hamlet*, read Müller's short text carefully and establish meaningful connections to the original, while also concentrating on *Hamletmachine*'s many points of departure from it. How does the postdramatic text converse with the original? Where does it break away from it? Does it question themes and topics present in the original? What other narratives are to be found in the postdramatic text?

- Look at the different media the postdramatic text uses and consider how they impact the reality of what spectators will see on stage. If you look at the recent production of *Hamlet* realized by the Wooster Group and toured all over the world, you will notice immediately that the project incorporates images from John Gielgud's 1964 Broadway production of *Hamlet*, starring Richard Burton in the title role. The theatrical performance was recorded by seventeen cameras and then edited into a movie shown in selected theatres. The Wooster Group wanted to create a diametrically opposite experience in "reconstructing a hypothetical theater piece from the fragmentary evidence of the edited film" (Wooster Group Website). The experiment raises pressing questions about archiving performance, the limits and possibilities of the theatrical medium, and the role of the text in the midst of different media. These are some issues you will have to ponder when dealing with an intermedial postdramatic performance: What are the connections between various forms of media? Are there hierarchies among the media displayed in the performance? What kind of aesthetic visions, or points of view, does the intersection of live theatre and recorded video bring about?

- Concentrate on the role of the performer's body and look at how it interfaces with the text. The body might have a language that transcends the text or that uses the text as either a commentary on the physical movements or simply as a displacing technique. In other cases, the text is simply not there, and all you have are tableaux and images. For instance, the sight of unsupervised toddlers in a glass cube in Romeo Castellucci's *Inferno* speaks louder than any text uttered in the performance, especially when you experience the small children's bodies under the threat of a dark cloud that is slowly engulfing them in its menacing embrace.

- Instead of relying on a cause-and-effect reading of the piece, allow for multiple and possibly disconnected narratives. Tune into a more sensorial approach and pay attention to how the piece creates a sense of mood and atmosphere.

- Consider your own engagement with the performance and reflect on your responsibility as a reader/dramaturg in shaping its meaning.

Practicum I

The following passage is from Act Three of Henrik Ibsen's *A Doll's House*. It is the end of the play and Torvald Helmer and Nora, husband and wife, are having a conversation about a woman's duties. Nora has previously stated that she must leave her family behind to find herself, and Helmer is trying to convince her to stay and abide by her assigned gender role and the social expectations that go with it. The final segment of the play can easily be misinterpreted as a conscious feminist statement on the part of the playwright, or as a militant stance from a woman who has understood her place in society and is ready to claim it. While there is clearly a change of mind in Nora that prompts her to separate from Helmer, the language she uses, combined with tone and structure of her lines, mitigate her resolution and show it as a necessary, yet difficult choice. Read the passage carefully and then answer briefly the following questions

HELMER   And I have to tell you that! Aren't they your duties to your husband and children?
NORA   I have other duties equally sacred.
HELMER   That isn't true. What duties are they?
NORA   Duties to myself.
HELMER   Before all else you are a wife and a mother.
NORA   I don't believe in that anymore. I believe that before all else, I'm a human being, no less than you—or anyway, I ought to try to become one. I know the majority thinks you're right, Torvald, and plenty of books agree with you, too. But I can't go on believing what the majority is saying, or what's written in books. I have to think over these things myself and try to understand them. (Roudané 276–277)

1. What is the major linguistic shift from Nora's first two lines to her third one?

2. In her third line, how does Nora manifest the difficult choice she is about to make?

3. What is the significance of the repetition of verbs such as "believe" and "try"?

4. How are we to understand Nora's sense of self in connection to her reference of "books" and the "majority" of people?

Practicum 2

Find in the dictionary the definition of the following common figures of speech, and provide one example for each of them in the space provided.

Metaphor:_____

_____

Example:_____

_____

Parallelism:_____

_____

Example:_____

_____

Analogy:_____

_____

Example:_____

_____

Simile:_____

_____

Example:_____

_____

Synecdoche:_____

_____

Example:_____

_____

Hyperbole:_____

_____

Example:_____

_____

Aphorismus:_____

_____

Example:_____

_____

Practicum 3

Aristotle admired Sophocles' *Oedipus the King* for its complex plot, its language, character, and the philosophical questions it asks. Read this exemplary tragedy with great attention and answer the following questions using the definition of tragedy provided in the previous chapter.

1. What is ironic about Oedipus' quest for justice?
2. What is Oedipus' *hamartia*? Try to move past the conventional answer that it is his arrogance. There is more to the character than his pride and egotism.
3. Where would you place the climax of the play?
4. What's the difference between the story and the plot of *Oedipus the King*?
5. How is *anagnorisis* connected to Oedipus' demise?
6. How does *miasma* manifest itself in the story? And how is it dealt with at the end of the play?
7. What is the moral lesson of the play?
8. Describe the feelings of "pity" and "fear" and explain briefly how they might manifest in the play?
9. Who would you say is Oedipus' antagonist?
10. Do some basic online research on the Oedipus' trilogy, and be ready to answer a few questions about the story of *Oedipus at Colonus* and *Antigone*.

CHAPTER 4

From Text to Performance

Reading a play can be challenging because it demands that the reader recreates the story in a visual way, but does so through linguistic means. Plays are also different from other literary narratives. The novel may rely on both direct and indirect speech to paint a very detailed picture of the characters and their background, and it allows for the story to move quickly from the past to the present and on to the future. The accumulation of details in the novel helps shape our understanding and reception of the story and reaches its goal in the act of reading. On the other hand, drama must wait for a production to fulfill its full communicative potential. Plays concede a lot less to their readers because they demand them to engage creatively to give life to the story and flesh out the characters. While one could argue that the action contained in the dramatic dialogue is in essence the most direct way to deliver the meaning of the story, that meaning is only fully achieved when it is experienced on stage. A play is always a work in progress because it never reaches its final form; its transient nature relies on the fact that it continues to tell the same story in different ways through the different productions the play will receive. Plays inherently demand to be staged continuously and always invite an active reading, a reading that is tied to the promise of a theatrical production.

This means that plays are bound by their ultimate destination: the stage. Everything that happens in a play must fit within what can be accomplished in the theatre and must account for the theatrical medium's limitations. However, when you read a play as a reader/ dramaturg for the first time, you should not be limited in your imagination and creativity by the space of the stage. Allow yourself to break free of the constraints a director might encounter when staging the play, and rather relish in the full realm of possibilities the text offers you. In subsequent readings, however, you should start reflecting on how the play might exist on a stage and what kind of theatrical space would prove the most suitable. A fully developed understanding of the play's characterization, super-objective, tone, genre, and visual and aural elements can help you make that decision.

In this chapter, we are going to engage with a number of reading strategies to help the reader/dramaturg experience the active nature of dramatic action.

Stage Directions

Many students believe a play's stage directions are not really significant and can be simply either skimmed over or skipped altogether. They believe that since a play's destiny is the stage, only the text spoken by the actors and heard by the audience should ultimately count. This misconception betrays both a dangerous mental laziness as well as a biased notion that putting up a theatrical representation is a straightforward operation where lines are memorized and delivered. My first reaction to the argument is "Why did the playwright bother to write stage directions if they are meaningless?" The second is "Can the stage directions lead to the analysis and understanding of the play?" Stage directions come in different forms and from different sources. It is important to determine whether they come from the playwright or from the first theatrical production of the play that has turned into the first published edition. This is relevant because, in the second case, the stage directions might communicate a reality tied to a specific directorial and design vision, and knowing that vision is intrinsic to the way the story has been told. If the playwright wrote them, the length and details of stage directions can inform readers about how the author envisioned the play as well as of her/his anxieties over the staging of the piece. Excessively long stage directions might be seen as an attempt to influence future productions and make sure her/his vision is not misinterpreted.

Regardless of whether they come from the playwright, however, stage directions are crucial clues to gain a more profound understanding of the play's world and the characters. They describe the physical reality of the play (e.g., country, city, room, style and décor, relations between objects and different spaces). They can also indicate characters' age and appearance, their movements, feelings, and voice quality, and their likes and dislikes. Stage directions can also suggest lighting cues and thus help the reader in following the story and making sense of scene changes. Finally, they might also point out relevant acting cues. The stage directions for Linda in the opening scene of *Death of a Salesman* immediately convey crucial aspects about her character and her relationship with her husband: ". . . she more than loves him, she admires him, as though his mercurial nature, his temper, his massive dreams and little cruelties, served her only as a sharp reminder of the turbulent longings within him, longings which she shares but lacks the temperament to utter and follow to their end" (Roudané 342). Miller has given us here a description of Linda as a representative of Cold War domesticity and active supporter of her husband. A few more acting directions in the scene consolidate Linda's supportive role as well as her lack of agency ("hearing Willy outside the bedroom, calls with some trepidation" "Very carefully, delicately," "helpfully," "resigned." Roudané 342–343). This is clearly vital information for someone who is not going to benefit from seeing a performance of the play and has to rely totally on the text to engage the story.

Let us consider the very long stage directions that premise Eugene O'Neill's *Long Day's Journey into Night* and see how they manage to convey not only the spatial reality of the play but also essential aspects of the characterization. This is an autobiographical play that was published after O'Neill's death, upon his own request. It describes the family of the playwright in great detail, so O'Neill felt that the staging had to do justice both to the characters and their dramatic circumstances. The stage directions provide many details such as the layout of the house, pictures on the wall, specific authors lining the bookcases, precise descriptions of types of furniture and its location in the house, and even the state of wear-and-tear of Shakespeare collections; but they also include characters' physical features, posture, style of clothes, movements and gestures, hair styles, and moral dispositions. It appears that O'Neill wanted future readers and spectators to really understand these characters on his own terms. His wish, however, is less important than the significance the stage directions have in helping us navigate the play. As a reader/dramaturg, you do not have to envision the setting and the characters as O'Neill wrote them in the stage directions, but you can surely draw on O'Neill's description to guide and direct your own vision, the same way that a director would approach the staging of the play.

The Theatre Space

As you read a play and start physicalizing the actions of the characters and envisioning the nature of the space, you should also start thinking about the kind of theatrical space that would best suit the play. While, most likely, you will not direct the play in your near future, it is a good exercise to consider the space that might host it because this allows you to think about the correlation existing between space and actions in the play and the kind of relationship you want to establish between the actors and the audience. You need to answer a number of important questions about the play to be able to make an informed decision about its staging: Whose story is it? Does the story have an intimate feel, or is it more conducive to the expression of big feelings? What would be the most appropriate type of delivery for the actors? Personal and intimate, or declamatory and loud? Would the audience enjoy being in closer proximity with the actors? Or would it prefer to observe the action from a distance? Does the play include direct address? Does it have a confessional tone? The way you answer each of these questions will inevitably inform your selection of a theatre space. These are your choices:

Proscenium: The audience sits in the auditorium, while the action happens on stage and is viewed as if through an invisible wall. The proscenium arch frames the action as "distant" from the reality of the spectators on stage. Whenever actors address the spectators directly, the illusion of the two distinct worlds is shattered, and people say that the actors broke the "fourth wall."

Thrust: In this configuration the stage juts out into the audience, literally thrusts itself, and spectators sit around three sides of it. This is a perfect space for intimate plays where the proximity of the audience is welcome.

Alley: In the alley theatre, spectators sit on two sides with the playing area in the middle. The viewing experience in the alley configuration is intimate, due to the close proximity of the actors, but it is also social because the audience members can see their fellow spectators at all times.

Arena: This is possibly the most challenging type of staging due to the fact that the audience surrounds the playing space on all sides. It is often used for large spectacular pieces where movement is continuous so that actors remain visible at all times.

Black Box: The most flexible of all theatre spaces, the black box theatre can be adapted to suit a variety of staging needs. The seating area can be arranged to simulate a thrust, proscenium, alley, or arena space, but it can also allow for novel and original spatial arrangements.

Sensory Experience

In their mission to bridge the gap between the page and the stage, the reader/dramaturgs bring to the reading experience not only their intellects but also their bodies. They engage the play text in a sensory fashion by trying to detect in it elements that awaken physical and corporeal reactions or by simply projecting onto the text a sensory response. We do this all the time when we read. Due to the fact that we understand simultaneously through our brain and our body, the act of reading engages both cognition and senses. Nevertheless, it can be hard to bring our senses to the reading of a play especially because we are getting more and more specific in our viewing habits and tend to connect more to audiovisual and digital narratives than traditional text-reading. However, there are strategies and methods that can make this task easier.

I am reminded of what Ignatius of Loyola, the founder of the Jesuit order, wrote in the sixteenth century in his *Spiritual Exercises*, a book dedicated to train novices and facilitate their meditation on biblical stories. Ignatius' suggestions belong in a dramaturgy book, because he views theatre as a means of education and proselytization. One of the exercises he uses is a meditation on hell, and for this task the student had to create a memory of hell through the use of all senses. Before starting the exercise, he had to recite a preparatory prayer, a first prelude where he would imagine hell in its "length, breadth, and depth," and a second prelude where he would ask for "an interior sense of the pain suffered by the damned." After this preparation, the student would meditate on five points:

> *The First Point* will be to see with the eyes of the imagination the huge fires and, so to speak, the souls within the bodies full of fire.
> *The Second Point.* In my imagination I will hear the wailing, the shrieking, the cries, and the blasphemies against our Lord and all his saints.
> *The Third Point.* By my sense of smell I will perceive the smoke, the sulphur, the filth, and the rotting things.
> *The Fourth Point.* By my sense of taste I will experience the bitter flavors of hell: tears, sadness, and the worm of conscience.
> *The Fifth Point.* By my sense of touch, I will feel how the flames touch the souls and burn them. (Loyola 46–47)

Each of these points was to be the object of the student's meditation until it became a permanent image, a memory that could be retrieved when needed to help the student on his spiritual path. The same level of commitment to the sensory exploration of the text presents itself in the prologue of William Shakespeare's *Henry V*. Here the Chorus lays out the theatrical conventions for the audience of the Globe theatre in London, explaining in detail the essential role of imagination and creativity in the understanding of the story:

O for a Muse of fire, that would ascend
The brightest heaven of invention,
A kingdom for a stage, princes to act,
And monarchs to behold the swelling scene!
Then should the warlike Harry, like himself,
Assume the port of Mars, and at his heels,
Leashed in like hounds, should famine, sword, and fire
Crouch for employment. But pardon, gentles all,
The flat unraised spirits that hath dared
On this unworthy scaffold to bring forth
So great an object. Can this cockpit hold
The vasty fields of France? Or may we cram
Within this wooden O the very casques
That did affright the air at Agincourt?
O, pardon! since a crooked figure may
Attest in little place a million,
And let us, ciphers to this great account,
On your imaginary forces work.
Suppose within the girdle of these walls
Are now confined two mighty monarchies,
Whose high upreared and abutting fronts
The perilous narrow ocean parts asunder.
Piece out our imperfections with your thoughts:
Into a thousand parts divide one man,
And make imaginary puissance.
Think, when we talk of horses, that you see them
Printing their proud hoofs i'th'receiving earth;
For 'tis your thoughts that now must deck our kings,
Carry them here and there, jumping o'er times,
Turning th'accomplishment of many years
Into an hour-glass: for the which supply,
Admit me Chorus to this story,
Who Prologue-like your humble patience pray,
Gently to hear, kindly to judge, our play.

Shakespeare emphasizes something quite simple: Imagination is the key to unlocking the full emotional impact of the story. Therefore, he invites the spectators to visualize characters and locales not as represented on stage, but as the byproduct of an imaginative exercise through which they could transcend and transform into mental narratives. The Elizabethan stage was quite simple in its use of design elements and props, so the audience of *Henry V* was accustomed to the conventions Shakespeare is describing. His words, however, are still resonant in today's world because they reiterate the creative activity theatregoers engage with every time they go to the theatre, no matter whether they watch a naturalistic performance, in which every attempt is made to reproduce a specific reality as it might present itself in daily life, or a more abstract play where realistic clues might be missing altogether. As human beings, we engage theatre in highly sophisticated ways through cognitive and sensorial processes that are meant to shape our understanding of a particular theatrical experience. We bring our past, present, and sense of the future into the theatre with us. We are willing to embark on a journey of discovery where we negotiate the representation of a foreign world written by the playwright and staged by a creative team of artists through our own sets of values and expectations.

The question I want to answer is whether we can transpose these imaginative and creative strategies into the act of reading a play. This is clearly a difficult proposition because as readers we experience the play firstly as a linguistic text. So, what are some techniques we can adopt to help us engage in the creative pursuit suggested by Shakespeare and Ignatius of Loyola? I am proposing a few exercises in the pages that follow, but the reality is that we all have our own creative strategies to bring the play text to life. Yours can be just as effective and useful.

Decorate the Space

Pick a few decorative elements you might find in the scene, and that might even be suggested in the stage directions, and situate them in the space you mentally create for the scene. Then envision how the characters might connect with those elements. If you are reading a scene set in a living room of a middle-class home, you might envision a sofa as part of the décor. What is the position of the characters in relation to the sofa? Are they sitting on it? Leaning on it? Hiding behind it? Reflect on the dramatic objectives of the characters in the scene and picture them as they move and interact within their space. As you progress in your reading, add more details to flesh out a fuller sense of the place: Include photos, artwork, lamps, and other objects; color the walls and envision design patterns; picture doors for entrances and exits; and think of how these things might affect how character use the space: Do they thwart characters' movement, or do they facilitate it? As you free your imagination, remember also to visualize the space according to what the characters say and do. If they discuss mixing a cocktail and smoking a cigar, most likely you will find yourself imagining the type of bar and the cigar box's position in the room. When envisioning the space and all other details of the play, begin with your own personal frames of reference. If you are reading Jean Paul Sartre's *No Exit*, for instance, it would be useful to do research on what a drawing-room in the Second Empire style looked like and reflect on how its overdecorated and sumptuous style might contribute to the oppressive feel of the room. However, for the first reading of the play, you can simply start by picturing your grandmother's old sofa. While accurate historical research is the bread and butter of any reader/dramaturg, as you read a play for the first time you should draw on your own personal experiences to make sense of the text.

Dress the Characters

When tackling a play, it is often difficult for inexperienced readers to perceive characters as more than disembodied voices or talking heads. It is essential, however, that you flesh out the characters visually if you aspire to fuel some life into them and, at the same time, make the reading more engaging for yourself. As I said earlier, the stage directions might tell you a lot about the characters' clothes, but you should not necessarily get bogged down by what the playwright wrote. Be creative in your envisioning of the characters, but also make sure that your vision is framed by the textual expectations of them. While a director might explore meaningful ways to subvert the given circumstances of characters in order to show how they might make sense in different cultural and aesthetic contexts, the reader/dramaturg has the responsibility to comprehend the play and its characters fully in their original incarnation. Any adaptive reading of the characters is highly desirable, but it should follow a contextual understanding of the play. You need to understand the play in its own terms, before you can adapt it.

More often than not, however, the play will not provide you with much information about what characters wear, and it is going to be your job to envision them. What I find useful in determining characters' clothing choices and styles is to think about their given circumstances. Are they rich or poor? What age are they? How's the weather? Where do they live? In what period? Are they trying to impress anybody? Is the scene outside or inside? And so on. I also try to determine where the characters are coming from and where they go after they leave the scene, and how their sense of self might reflect what they decide to wear. You don't have to envision all of their clothes; you can start with a small detail that helps you characterize them in a meaningful way, and incorporate that detail into your mental staging of the scene. This exercise can work with clothes the play mentions in the scene, or with imaginary ones that you see fit for the characters to wear.

Block the Scene

Since its origin, theatre has always been associated with the staging of characters' actions contained within the temporal and spatial frame of the representation. Avant-garde theatre has experimented with characters speaking their lines without ever moving, but we seldom consider verbal communication as separate from physical action. Reading a play is always an exercise in enacting and staging characters' actions. When you read a play, you want to imagine it in the most dynamic way possible, and there are strategies you can use to "move" the characters so that they might emerge more vividly from the page.

Regardless of whether the play suggests it, you should imagine that your characters come into the scene from somewhere else and always go somewhere else at the end of it. They are mobile rather than stuck. The play might not tell you where they were and where they are going, but it is a meaningful exercise to investigate their provenance and destination so as to sketch them out in a more detailed fashion. I am not suggesting inventing the given circumstances of the character, but rather analyzing them thoroughly so that you can make intelligent guesses.

Picturing a character's movement is often embedded in the language she/he speaks as well as in the circumstances of the scene. Look for the active verbs and reflect on whether they might carry physical actions, but also avoid obvious choices. A character might want to run away, but maybe that's not possible due to the social setting and physical confinement of the scene. The struggle to stay put might emerge more powerfully through controlled demeanor, rather than erratic and agitated behavior. The key to a character's movement might be provided by the subtext of the scene, so be discerning in your imagined blocking. A character's objectives and super-objective are the lenses through which movement should be framed. The difficult, yet rewarding, task of envisioning movement lies in finding the balance between what the play provides you with in terms of characterization and given circumstances, and your ability to interpret them creatively.

In determining how characters move on stage, make sure you consider that each body is conditioned by the time in which it lives, its gender, its class and status, its wealth, and other attributes. How characters move is a complex riddle to solve, and it hinges on their social mores, the cultural forces that shape how they act and are acted upon, their environment, and gender-specific expectations. You do not have the same body, or the same mind, of someone who lived in Athens in the fourth century B.C.E. You have to reconstruct what it might have been like to be Jason and Medea in Euripides' tragedy, and inhabit their bodily reality. Once we have a clearer notion of the physical reality of the characters, you can start teasing out how to bring those realities to life through movement and blocking.

Objects and Their Sensory Allure

In his landmark philosophical treatise *Meditations on First Philosophy*, Rene Descartes comments on how "things" evolve and develop into different forms and adapt due to shifting temporal and spatial conditions and framing devices. Using his observation of beeswax, Descartes reflects on how things have the power to retain some of their original characteristics even when they mutate into different shapes and forms. The philosopher wants to underline how the properties of things are grounded in object-relations that create networks of significations that might be difficult to detect at a first glance but that are, nevertheless, foundational to the life of the object in question:

> Let us, for example, take this wax: it has only just been removed from the honeycomb; it has not lost yet all the flavor of its honey; it retains some of the scent of the flowers among which it was gathered; its color, shape, and size

are clearly visible; it is hard, cold, easy to touch, and if you tap it with your knuckle, it makes a sound. In short, it has all the properties that seem to be required for a given body to be known as distinctly as possible. But wait—while I am speaking, it is brought close to the fire. The remains of its flavor evaporate; the smell fades; the color is changed, the shape is taken away, it grows in size, becomes liquid, becomes warm, it can hardly be touched, and now, if you strike it, it will give off no sound. Does the same wax still remain? We must admit it does remain: no one would think or say it does not. (22)

Descartes continues discussing the beeswax to prove that intellectual understanding supersedes sensorial perception, but we want to stop at his reflection about the nature of things and their power to suggest and evoke different and distant images. But why is this so important to someone who wants to read a play? More importantly, why should a reader bother with delving into the more recondite and sophisticated layers of a given image or object?

The objects that appear in plays, and that become props in the staging, may have literal and symbolical meanings. They make sense as literal objects, while also serving as tools to deflect, project, and suggest different meanings. Let's reflect briefly on the value that the skull of Yorick, the court jester, has in *Hamlet*.

Alas, poor Yorick! I knew him, Horatio, a fellow of infinite jest, of most excellent fancy. He hath bore me on his back a thousand times, and now how abhorr'd in my imagination it is! My gorge rises at it. Here hung those lips that I have kiss'd I know not how oft. Where be your gibes now, your gambols, your songs, your flashes of merriment, that were wont to set the table on a roar? Not one now to mock your own grinning—quite chop-fall'n. (Roudané 183)

Seeing the skull reminds Hamlet of his own childhood and spurs his consideration of mortality as great social equalizer and oblivion:

No, faith, not a jot, but to follow him thither with modesty enough and likelihood to lead it: Alexander died, Alexander was buried, Alexander returneth to dust, the dust is earth,

of earth we make loam, and why of that loam whereto he
was converted might they not stop a beer-barrel?
Imperious Caesar, dead and turn'd to clay,
Might stop a hole to keep the wind away.
O that that earth which kept the world in awe
Should patch a wall t'expel the [winter's] flaw! (Roudané 183)

Yorick's skull fits well with the theme of the play, with its
mood, and its general atmosphere of mourning and revenge. The
reader perceives the skull as a vivid metaphor for death in general:
Hamlet's father's, Ophelia's premature disappearance, the violent
deaths of Polonius, Rosencrantz, and Guildenstern, and all the
dead bodies that will pile up by the end of the play. It also provides
an interesting commentary on Hamlet's characterization because
it allows him to verbalize his own convictions about mortality and
life after death. More importantly, the skull produces a series of
other images that are central to the play. First, Hamlet creates a list
of all the facial parts that are missing from it and, by doing so, literally reconstructs Yorick's face for the reader and the spectator. We
are encouraged to picture these missing parts, to imagine what the
jester might have looked like when Hamlet was a child. Second, as
Yorick's skull is stripped of all personal details and specificity, it
conveys a quite generic view of humanity, and it is for this reason
that it can move from the sphere of personal memories (the jester of
Hamlet's own childhood) to that of a collective mankind. In the context of Hamlet's speech, the skull conjures up the powerful images
of Alexander and Caesar, but within the context of life's inescapable destiny. The skull is a visual and metaphorical reminder of the
meaning of living and dying. Shakespeare did not need to include
Yorick's skull to comment on mortality, but the presence of the skull
acts as a powerful catalyst because it represents what death leaves
behind while at the same time providing a visual reminder of a
vacated life. It coalesces the temporal frames of the play and presents a physical focus for Hamlet's philosophical ruminations.

When reading a play, dramaturgs must consider how objects
have multiple functions. They can be taken at face value by looking at what immediate purpose they serve in the play (a sword will
always be a sword!), but they also provide alternative meanings
and sensorial responses (e.g., a sword can be a phallic symbol, a
stand in for war and the military). In the case mentioned above,
Yorick's skull has an immediate meaning of being part of Hamlet's
old friend's mortal remains, but it also stands as a metaphor for

mortality. To return to Descartes' example of the beeswax, the skull is malleable and permeable to our interpretations. It allows the reader to perceive at once Hamlet's happy childhood, the uncertainty of his present, and the inescapable doom of his future.

As a reader/dramaturg, you should also consider how objects/props affect the reality of the character. The skull that Hamlet handles has weight, texture, color, and possibly the scent of wet soil and decaying bodies that one might smell in a cemetery. These are impacting qualities that might elicit feelings of repulsion or even horror in most people. Being aware of them can help you create a vivid image of the scene and a more complete analysis of Hamlet's state of mind in this situation.

The reader/dramaturg endows the objects in the play text as existing both inside and outside the world of the play, as real and symbolic. Let's consider the pen Biff steals in *Death of a Salesman* and reflect on how this object functions in the text. We do not doubt that Biff stole a real pen: He confesses to it; it is an episode other characters discuss; it is an action that brings about Biff's awareness that he cannot live his father's dream of success but has to find his own. Nevertheless, the pen also comments on facets of Biff's character that are less evident. While stealing a pen might be a crime of opportunity for him (he is alone for a moment and he steals the least voluminous object he can find in the office), it is also true that the pen represents a life that is outside of Biff's experience, and that is to him, at least in the specific moment, very appealing. The pen exemplifies the security of an office job that Biff would like in order to give meaning to his life and to please his father. It also conjures up a life of the mind, a professional job one acquires through years of study and hard work. This is clearly connected to Biff's decision to flunk math and consequently forfeit his chance to study at the University of Virginia. Finally, the pen as a tool to record and pass on one's own voice and opinions, to have a voice and agency, may express Biff's desperate desire to communicate his feelings, something he has been incapable of achieving up until this point.

Concentrating on what objects mean in a play is an excellent exercise to decipher dramaturgical nuances that one might miss otherwise. How characters handle objects and how they make them part of their actions is also an interesting thing to observe because it might speak directly to the play's theme. Lope de Vega's religious drama *La Mayor Corona* narrates the story of Hermenegildo, a prince who died for his faith in the sixth century. The play wants to prove that the major crown (*la mayor corona*) is the one granted at death when the faithful is awarded eternal life in heaven, as opposed to the literal crown that adorns the head of the king. In order to prove the insubstantial nature of the monarchical crown, Lope depicts it as it moves from head to head, physically suggesting its inconsistency and unreliability. Reflect on a second example from Shakespeare's *Othello*. The handkerchief that Othello gives to Desdemona, and that Emilia finds and gives to her husband Iago, is more than a prop used to convince Othello that Desdemona has been unfaithful to him with Cassio. Not only is the handkerchief refined and beautifully embroidered, it also comes with the prophecy that once lost, it will bring about the end of love between husband and wife. Othello reminds Desdemona of what the Egyptian fortune teller who had crafted the handkerchief had told his mother: "if she lost it / Or made gift of it, my father's eye / Should hold her loathed." (87) In the famous Shakespearian tragedy, the handkerchief is a literal representation of marital (in)fidelity: The fact that it belonged to Othello's mother places it in the sacred realm of the family unit, but as it passes from hand to hand, the handkerchief takes on darker meaning and could signify that the purity of marriage is tainted by corruption, real and imagined, and by mistrust.

It is quite important at this point to expand on the notion of objects in theatre through the theory of object-relationship of Melanie Klein (1882–1960), a psychoanalyst who made a name for herself in Europe and the United States due to her studies of how people form attachments to specific objects and decide to represent them in different contexts. Her complex theories are situated within Freudian psychology and the study of phenomena of transference, but what should interest you, as a reader/dramaturg, is the fact that Klein expands the signification of objects beyond mere inanimate objects. Robert Blumenfeld, in his landmark book *Tools and Techniques for Character Interpretation*, illustrates Klein's ample definition of object:

> The underlying idea of object-relations theory is a simple one: we are always in some relationship to objects. The word *object* most often means a person, although it also means a place, thing, or any external or internal matter for contemplation. It also may refer to the self: the self as internal object, meaning the self objectified, externalized, and held up to the light, so to speak, so that we can examine it. Both conscious and unconscious self-images are objects. (90)

Not only does Klein open up the definition of object to include people, she also applies the term to the notion of self in order to illustrate how a person might form an object-relation with her-/ himself. When you apply her theories to the reading of plays, you might find they are useful to reflect on how characters relate to other characters in the play and to self-made images of themselves as objects they manipulate and with whom they interact. Do they project unusual meanings onto others? What kind of vision of themselves do they have? Is it a realistic and/or objective vision? Can you extrapolate by how they act whether the relationships they form with others are grounded in misconceptions, fabrications of imaginary realities, or simply whether they are fully aware of the kind of world they inhabit? If, as Klein argued, people construct mental representations of objects and relate to these representations instead of to the objects themselves, one can gather that objects are always the result of attribution of values and thus loaded with significations to unpack. Analyzing characters' rapport with their principal objects can unlock novel ways to understand them.

As an example, consider Blanche DuBois in *A Streetcar Named Desire*, one of Tennessee Williams' most famous plays. She is a woman in her thirties with a traumatic past, full of secrets. Since she cannot face her reality, she escapes into a world of fantasy and delusions of grandeur. She identifies with an image of herself that is at odds with both her present situation and the perception others have of her. The image she has constructed of a proper, modest, and attractive woman in the prime of her life is an object that exists merely as a projection, as a totally fabricated idea of self. To avoid facing her past and the lies she has told everybody, she retreats further into the past, to an internal vision of herself that is as captivating as it is heartbreaking to watch for the audience. In the following lines it is evident how she constructed herself as an object, and the fact that she is fully aware of her construction: "I don't want realism. I want magic! (*Mitch laughs*) Yes, yes, magic! I try to give that to people. I misrepresent things to them. I don't tell truth, I tell what *ought* to be truth. And if that is sinful, then let me damned for it!" (117). When Mitch, the man whom Blanche hopes will propose to her, finds out about Blanche's shady past and accuses her of lying, she candidly replies "Never inside, I didn't lie in my heart" (119). For a reader/dramaturg, it would be quite crucial to figure out what vision of herself Blanche harbors and what that means in the economy of the play's theme and structure. Researching notions of Southern social behavior and decorum, as well as the position of single women in that society would be necessary first steps to understand Blanche's constructed self.

Practicum I

Read scene seven of *The Glass Menagerie* and try to experience it from a sensory standpoint. Following both the stage directions and the textual clues, imagine what it might feel like for Laura to be alone with Jim, the young man she has loved since her childhood, and to experience such strong emotions after having led a life of longing and solitude. As you answer the questions below, put yourself in Laura's position and imagine how her feelings might be evolving at different moments in the scene.

- What is the temperature in the room? How does it affect Laura?
- How does it feel to go from the brightness of electrical lighting to the moody quality of candlelight? Take in what the room might feel like in the semi-darkness. Consider what can be seen clearly and what is either shadowy or unseen.
- Is it comfortable sitting on the floor? Does it make Laura feel more or less vulnerable?
- How does her new dress feel on her skin?
- What is the layout and décor of the Wingfield apartment? Do they affect how Laura might feel about herself?
- What is the smell in the apartment? Does it come only from the food, or is there a distinctive smell to the place?
- What kind of sounds can be heard in and outside the apartment? How does it feel for Laura to hear them?
- How does the dandelion wine taste?
- How does the chewing gum taste? How does it affect the way she speaks?
- How much can Laura see of Jim through the candlelight?
- How does the candlelight affect Laura's behavior (her shyness, her motions, the way she talks)?
- How does it feel to be touched by Jim when they dance? What about being kissed?
- What does the sound of the crashing unicorn feel like to Laura?

Practicum 2

Following the stage geography below, write down characters' blocking in scene five of Act Three of *Hamlet*. This is the beginning of the confrontation between Gertrude and Hamlet, leading up to Polonius' murder. The stakes are really high, because the hero is in an excited state of mind, and the queen appears to be concerned about her well-being and that of her only son.

- Pay attention to what the language suggests in terms of movement, but draw on your own creative interpretation to block the scene.
- Write down the movement directly in the text using the abbreviations suggested in the chart.
- At the end of the exercise, explain briefly the choices you made.

UR (Upstage Right)	UC (Upstage center)	UL (Upstage Left)
R (Right)	C (Center)	L (Left)
DR (Downstage Right)	DC (Downstage Center)	DL (Downstage Left)

HAMLET: Now, mother, what's the matter?
QUEEN: Hamlet, thou hast thy father much offended.
HAMLET: Mother, you have my father much offended.
QUEEN: Come, come, you answer with an idle tongue.
HAMLET: Go, go, you question with a wicked tongue.
QUEEN: Why, how now, Hamlet?
HAMLET: What's the matter now?
QUEEN: Have you forgot me?
HAMLET: No, by the rood, not so:
          You are the Queen, your husband's brother's wife,
          And would it were not so, you are my mother.
QUEEN: Nay, then I'll set those to you that can speak.

HAMLET: Come, come, and sit you down, you shall not boudge;
You go not till I set you up a glass
Where you may see the [inmost] part of you.

QUEEN: What will thou do? Thou wilt not murther me?
Help ho! (Roudané 148)

Conclusion

The dramaturg's duties highlighted in the introduction can suggest reading strategies grounded in creativity and imagination to the reader/dramaturg who is trying to find meaningful ways to understand a play. These strategies come to fruition before, during, and after reading a play and are meant both to expand the reader/dramaturg's knowledge of the play script and to probe viable visions to stage it. The following chart illustrates how a reader/dramaturg can follow in the footsteps of a professional production dramaturg.

Dramaturg's Duties	Practical Suggestions for Reader/Dramaturgs
Research the world of the play	Go to see the play in the theatre, if you can, but in the absence of a live performance, concentrate on cinematic renditions or videos of theatrical productions posted on YouTube. Conduct research on the time and place of the play, and the sociocultural elements that contributed to shaping it. Collect audio and visual materials that exemplify the given circumstances of the play and use these tools to contextualize your own understanding of the storyline and characters.
Compile glossaries of difficult and/or foreign words	Make a list of all the terms you do not know and research them online or at the library. Make notes on the margin of the text, so that on a second reading of the play you can understand the problematic word in its context.

(continued)

Dramaturg's Duties	Practical Suggestions for Reader/ Dramaturgs
Answer the question "Why should this play be staged?"	Think of the play's themes and characters and ask how they resonate in today's culture. Question whether there are interest groups that might specifically find the play appealing. Is it a play with strong female characters? Does it portray a particular ethnic or cultural group? Does it engage ideas that are current in sociocultural discourses?
Production history	Check what aspects/themes of the play theatre directors explored in past productions. Find reviews and check how they describe the *mise en scène* and reflect on whether they match your own vision, or whether they can help you refine your original ideas about the play. Use them as a tool to explore and deepen your analysis, but do not let them sidetrack your own intuitions and interpretations. Use the reviews to support your arguments but be willing to consider and accept other interpretations if they are sound and convincing.
Dramaturgical notes for the program	Writing allows the dramaturg to speak directly to the audience. It is usually through the notes that she/he provides the spectators with tools such as critical analysis of the play, explanation of production's values, historical timeline, brief information about the playwright, and other useful ways to contextualize the current production. As an exercise, compose a written report as a response to the play. It does not have to be academic in nature, but it should contain some indication of why you feel this play deserves a production.

Dramaturg's Duties	Practical Suggestions for Reader/ Dramaturgs
Collaborate with the theatre's marketing personnel to develop strategies to bring audiences into the theatre	Think of a central image that can encapsulate either the main theme or the essential dramatic drive of the play, and find images that can represent them. Draw a poster or collect images that might do justice to the play. For instance, what images could best represent *Antigone*? Furthermore, think of ways to engage the audience. Are there specific groups that might find this play interesting? What can you do to promote the play to these groups?
Curate lobby display	One task dramaturgs often take on before the show opens is that of curating a lobby display that might include a variety of documents about the playwright, the play, the rehearsal process, archival objects, images, artifacts, maps, pictures, and documents. You will not have a theatre lobby to curate, but you can engage in a similar exercise by choosing three "things" that you might decide to include in a display to describe the play. You are now allowing your creativity to run free, so think as if you have a real theatre to fill and no budget to constrain you.
Run talkback sessions	Dramaturgs answer questions from the audience or direct these questions to the director and the actors. In their function as facilitators, they allow for the rich culture that produced the staged play to emerge, discuss organically the journey from text to performance, and confront firsthand the impact the play has had on the

(continued)

Dramaturg's Duties	Practical Suggestions for Reader/ Dramaturgs
	public. While organizing and running a talkback is not a feasible exercise for a student who is just reading a play for class, there are two things you can try that would simulate a talkback scenario. Craft three questions that you believe would stimulate a public discussion and ask them to your classmates during a formal in-class presentation.
Archive all dramaturgical material	The final task of the dramaturg, after the post mortem for the show is over, is to archive all the research she/he has gathered and shared so that it might be available for future reference. As a class exercise, you will submit a folder that includes all your dramaturgical findings. It should have at least the following items: a brief description of what value the play has in the current world, a short biography of the playwright, some reviews of significant productions of the play that have occurred in the last ten to fifteen years, visual documentation that illustrates the given circumstances of the play, and some research that speaks to the characters' world. As an alternative to the physical packet, you can create a digital file on the social network "Tumblr" including all the material listed above. Make sure you email the link for the webpage to both your instructor and classmates.

Interview

This interview with Kim McCaw about New Play Dramaturgy was conducted on September 11, 2012, and transcribed on February 27, 2013.

MUNERONI: Kim, can you explain how you got interested in dramaturgy and the kind of work you do in this field?

MCCAW: I do have a lot of experience in the field of dramaturgy, and I think I'm certainly not unique for my generation. I spent a major part of my life working in the development and production of new plays in that I'm as much a director as I am a dramaturg. Many times, in the development of the new work that I have done, I have been both director and dramaturg at the same time. It's only really been in more recent years that I have had some occasions to work as a dramaturg only and not as a director, and I've only had a few occasions to be a director where I've had a dramaturg working with me. I really enjoyed those experiences, and in fact probably the most important one was when I became the artistic director of the Prairie Theatre Exchange in Winnipeg in 1983. That was a company that really had as a central focus the production of new plays, new plays from the Prairies, and new plays from Manitoba especially. I didn't have a lot of experience in that area: My prior work had been at the Globe Theatre in Regina, doing a lot of new work, but a lot of it was children's theatre and a few new plays. So I contracted Per Brask, a Danish fellow at the University of Winnipeg—he's still there—who trained as a dramaturg in Europe in the European tradition of dramaturgy, but who's also a playwright and a writer. He worked with me for a couple of seasons as our playwright/dramaturg, and he was absolutely invaluable. When his time at the university changed, and I moved on, he stopped being the theatre's regular dramaturg, but I give him a lot of credit for teaching me a great deal about it. Some of our more interesting work happened in those early days. One of the things I really am proud of was working with Patrick Friesen, a poet at that time based in Winnipeg and who lives in Vancouver now. He had written a long dramatic poem called *The Shunning*, which dealt with an incident in a Mennonite community in rural Manitoba, and a publisher in the city gave me the text and said, "I think this could make a really exciting piece of theatre"—similar to Michael Ondaatje's *The Collected Works of Billy the Kid*, if you're familiar with that. So I read it, and I agreed, but I was not sure how we were going to make to happen. So we approached Patrick, and he was excited about collaborating on the project, and Per Brask got involved, so the three of us kind of worked together on it. And what we ended up with was one of the most exciting shows we ever did there, and interestingly enough it was revived a year or so ago on the main stage at the Manitoba Theatre Center. Another significant piece we developed at Prairie Theatre Exchange was a collaboration between our company and the French language theatre in the city, Le Cercle Molière. It dealt with the big turmoil that happened in Manitoba at one point over minority language rights. In colonial time Manitoba was a French language community and then things started to change and French became a minority language and there was a lot of trouble in the community about this. I decided we needed to do some kind of a show about it and it became ultimately a political cabaret. I also realized that it had to have involvement from the French community. So I approached the French theatre—they were a little bit apprehensive at first but I was able to gain their trust and we decided to jointly produce the show. And it would end up being a production in their season, and then a production in my season, literally going across the river kind of thing. And it was written by a team of writers, an Anglophone and a Francophone and then a bilingual song writer. It was written originally in English, then translated into French, but we rehearsed it first in French, and performed it in French. The moment that it opened in French we went back into the rehearsal hall to re-stage it in English. So the actors were performing in French at night, and acting in English during the day. Then we ran it in English at our theatre and shot a French television version of it. Anyway, Per Brask was again a key dramaturg for this project, which dealt with politics, language politics, and bilingualism. We described the play in my theatre as being in English with occasional French and it was the other way around in the other one.

MUNERONI: It seems that a dramaturg is someone who can wear many hats: director, researcher, facilitator, language expert. Would you say that this is your experience? These kinds of fluid professional skills?

McCAW: For sure. When I teach dramaturgy now, I start from the point of view that dramaturgs are "readers," and readers in the broadest definition of the term reading. It starts with their ability to read the play on the page, understand it, and imagine it much like a director or a designer perhaps, to imagine it as a performance. But it's also the ability—and this is where it gets more interesting—to read a production as it's developing, to listen to a read-through and hear nuances, and to watch a rehearsal develop. For example, during rehearsal you watch a scene and you can go to the director afterwards and say, "You know when we worked on this scene earlier we thought that these were the important parts of the scene and the scene was about such and such. When I watched it today, I'm seeing other things. I'm seeing this and that and the other. Is that what you meant?" That's about reading as well. If I'm involved in a production, I do this whether I work with the playwright or a director. And then I guess when I'm wearing both the dramaturgical and directorial hats, I'm trying to talk to myself *(laughs)* and, as long as I listen, I'm okay.

MUNERONI: The way we teach play analysis in the university sometimes is very literal; it's often all about the dramatic text. To me the perspective of the dramaturg is essential because it does bring into focus the reading of the play as well as its staging. I think this is what we should be teaching in the play analysis class. Can you expand on how you read a play when you are a dramaturg or a director/dramaturg?

McCAW: There are a few really simple things I do. If it's a play I've never read, and I focus primarily on new plays that have never been produced before, I try very hard to organize my time so that I read the play all in one sitting. I do that because an audience is going to sit down and watch it (hopefully) in one sitting, and so I want to share that same experience. The first time through I'm mostly looking to be entertained. I'm looking to enjoy going through the text. I want to find out all the really basic stuff: what happens next, whether there's something about the story that I find exciting or interesting, whether there's a character who really captures my imagination, and whether I care about the situation. Then it starts to become more detailed. I think I work from a kind of political perspective to a certain extent—not a hardcore one, but I do have a probably left of center perspective on a lot of things, so if the play isn't attempting to engage in some way with the world that we're in (even if it's a play from another time), if I can't see a relevance and a value to the play to here and now, I will probably have less interest in it. I'm also keen on the sense of theatricality and in writers who are interested in things that can happen on a stage as opposed to other forms of written communication. Are there believable characters? Is there dialogue that sounds like the way human beings talk? Again this is based on plays that are coming out of a fairly conventional set of values and goals and stuff. It becomes different if you're working with a writer who might want to push into other kinds of territory and is not working with conventional realism.

MUNERONI: Could you elaborate on the kinds of research you conduct on the play's references, historical and social/political times and then how you relate your findings to the director, the actors, and the creative team?

McCAW: Well, I guess if we're looking at plays that are attempting to be truthful to a time, to a community, or to an issue, it's important for me to know things that relate to those issues. If it's dealing with a particular political event, or a social event, let's say, a community event, then I need to research that event beyond what the play tells me, if for no other reason than to make sure that the play is reasonably accurate in its interpretation or its portrayal, or if it's deliberately trying to do a different spin on it, or comment on it. That's great, and that can be really exciting, but then we have to know—how is the audience going to know that? It also affects design choices to a certain extent. Many years ago, I went to see a new play in Winnipeg, and the play took place in 1967 in the backyard of a hippie commune in Vancouver, and it had to be 1967 because the whole plot revolved around going to Expo 67 in Montreal. It was about a bunch of stoned out hippies, so they had psychedelic art on the back and on the front of the house there was spray painted graffiti-style a reproduction of the cover of the *Abbey Road* album of the Beatles, the one with the group members walking across the road. The problem is that the album came out only in 1969 *(laughs)*. And then there was a picture from the *Yellow Submarine* album which came out in 1968, so I left the show at intermission because I couldn't believe anything about that show. This was a case of dramaturgy betraying the design, which resulted in a dishonest production. And I guess that's ultimately another thing that I'm looking for in terms of a playwright, when I'm reading a play, that sense of honesty, that sense of authenticity. Does this person really understand the play that he/she is writing here? Are they actually speaking from some central part of themselves, or are they just faking it?

MUNERONI: Can you describe the relationship you establish with the playwright in the context of new play dramaturgy? What would you define as a nurturing meaningful relationship? I'm sure you've had very good ones and very bad ones.

McCAW: I think there is a kind of unequivocal commitment to one another. I have a couple of playwrights in particular with whom I have had relatively long-term and productive artistic relationships. Wendy Lil was one; we did a number of her plays at Prairie Theatre Exchange. They were really our signature pieces and it was largely because Wendy was working from a sociopolitical sensibility that I completely understood, and was excited by, and I was completely committed to her. And again wearing more than one hat, I was the artistic director of the theatre too, so what I had the ability to do was to say to Wendy, "I'll give you money to write another play, and I will do it." I understood how she worked, I understood how she wrote, and she was able to listen to me, and I was able to say things that helped her. So it was just a tremendously productive relationship. Don Hannah is another writer I was excited to collaborate with. He's a very different writer than Wendy, but again he's a writer who I think that I get. And I think this is really important. There are some writers that you get and there are some writers that you appreciate, and as far as Don is concerned I read his work and I go, "Oh, yeah. That makes so much sense to me. I know how this play works; I understand who these characters are; I know how this is supposed to come to life on stage."

MUNERONI: Does it make a big difference when you appreciate, or even love, the work of a playwright?

McCAW: Yeah. If the playwrights don't believe that you believe in their play, then it's hard for them to accept criticism, I guess. It's kind of a dishonest relationship to have, if the message they're getting is that you really think the play is not really worth doing, but "here's a few things you could try." So yeah, I try and work from a point of view of believing in the play. I never try to tell them how to change it, I try and tell them what I see, and where I have questions, and when I get confused because the subject changes suddenly. So it can be very structural, but it can also be very intuitive.

MUNERONI: In new play dramaturgy, the dramaturg is also approaching the role of the creator somehow. There is something very artistic in being able to provide a playwright with a kind of a witnessing interface that allows for the articulation of new ideas. This does not happen in production dramaturgy!

McCAW: You can't talk to the playwright if she/he is dead.

MUNERONI: Right. But even when she/he is alive, I rarely have any interaction with the playwright. So this is something very interesting and I think it's one of the major differences maybe between production and new play dramaturgy.

McCAW: Well, a really interesting book, and you are probably familiar with it, is *Letters to George*. It's very interesting because Max Stafford-Clark had to work on George Farquhar and realized that it had been decades since he had worked without a living playwright, so he kind of brought George back to life as it were. Something else I wanted to talk about in terms of relationship to playwrights is that one of the things I will do with playwrights is to establish places where I will meet with them, and I will always ask them, "let's go for lunch or something . . . you pick the place." In Winnipeg I was working with a number of different writers, and I was always careful to never take them to the same place. I never wanted Patrick Friesen to see me with Ian Ross. I joke about it: "He knows I'm seeing other people, but I don't want to flaunt it" *(laughs)*.

MUNERONI: Yes, the bond of trust . . .

McCAW: There was a certain lousy Chinese restaurant that I would meet with Patrick Friesen, there was a certain coffee shop pool hall I would meet with Ian Ross. It was really . . . there is a different relationship, it isn't a cookie cutter thing.

MUNERONI: With the Canadian Centre for Theatre Creation, you dealt with the function of the dramaturg as speaker to the society at large. You organized public talks with playwrights that were staging their shows at the Citadel Theatre or in other theatres in town, and with Nobel laureates such as Derek Walcott. How important is it for you, as a dramaturg, to reach out to the population at large, rather than just the ones that come to the theatre to attend the show?

McCAW: Well, I think our job is to try and engage our communities in the theatrical work that we're doing, in as many ways as we can. Partly because I'm simply in awe of writers for the theatre, I think that there is something amazing about that particular artistry, and so I celebrate it. Those talks allowed me to share these writers and find a way for them to talk about their work. Hopefully somebody is going to be excited by something they heard, and maybe they'll come and see either that particular writer's work or that of another writer. Ultimately we are in a bit of an evangelical game to spread the word of theatre, in whatever form it is. I don't expect everybody to be excited by that particular group of writers, but hopefully one or two of them will be.

MUNERONI: What is it that might trigger a dramaturgical interest in a first-year student taking a play analysis class? Moreover, do you have any advice for someone who is just now starting to read about plays and would like to become a dramaturg?

McCAW: Well, I think the first part of that question is tricky. Many people come into the theatre, whether it's as a kid or as a high school and college student, as an actor. The actor is often the way in. But many aren't ultimately actors, they're readers. So I would say you read, and then if you are starting to become interested in this notion of new work, find the places in your community where new plays are being done. It can be a full-scale institution theatre, but again if you look around you'll see independent productions, there are little festivals, almost every city has some kind of mini festival of new work of some form. Approach them, get involved with them, talk to them. Almost no theatre organization is ever going to say no to somebody who comes and says "Can I do something?" (laughs). Find a playwright, get to be their friend, find a writer who gets you excited and help them.

MUNERONI: What about pursuing an MFA in dramaturgy?

McCAW: Very few theatres are in the position of hiring a full-time dramaturg. So I would encourage MFA graduates to learn some aspects of publicity, marketing, and audience development. Activities that dramaturgs can pursue cross into that territory, whether it be developing program material, creating a talkback series, or organizing various kinds of outreach activities. Develop some transferable skills that they will actually pay you for. Theatres do hire those people, and if you're around, then you can get into the rehearsals, you can get access to the director and the artists.

MUNERONI: Thank you for your time, Kim.

McCAW: My pleasure.

This interview with Dr. Colleen Reilly was conducted via email correspondence and was delivered on September 24, 2013.

MUNERONI: Colleen, can you briefly describe what dramaturgy means to you?

REILLY: Dramaturgy is a creative process that links a production to both the world of the play and to its eventual audience. The world of the play can encompass the language, imagery, historical context, production history, and the playwright's larger concerns. The audience cannot only include a specific population or demographic, but also an imagined ideal spectator. Dramaturgy is also a collaborative process of demystifying the elements of a production that could get in the way of the creative process while preserving the integrity of the production choices.

In other words, I see dramaturgy as a kind of "production whispering." The dramaturg's role is to see that nothing gets in the way of the production's best self and to identify strategies to remove any obstacles that stall the creative process. This can mean investigating questions posed by the director, providing context for the actors, supporting the research of the designers, and anticipating the needs or desires of the audience. I do not think it is possible for a dramaturg to have a one-size-fits-all approach to production, because each collaboration is unique and every creative project invites a different kind of inquiry.

MUNERONI: Can you illustrate in a few words how you arrived to the practice of dramaturgy, and how it enhanced your directorial vision?

REILLY: I would describe myself as an instinctual dramaturg. I used dramaturgical techniques as a director before I knew what to call them. I have always leaned toward "auteur" or "devised" theatre and was heavily influenced by it in a production that I wrote, directed, and performed in for the Piccolo Spoleto Fringe Festival in Charleston, South Carolina. I collaborated with actors, musicians, and a shadow puppeteer and found as a director that I was serving more of an editorial function. I had created a text, and there were so many strong ideas and points of view that came forward from the individual disciplines around that central idea. The rehearsal process became about weighing choices and negotiating not only how they "felt" in the world of the production, but also what their cumulative effect was becoming. We simply could not decide how to stage the final scene and concluded that it was best to stage it twice in succession with different endings. Our problem was that we wanted the audience to stay in an ambiguous place while still concluding the action of the play. For me, that production choice was essentially dramaturgical. The play called for it. The production called for it. The collaborators called for it. And, in the end, the audience called for it.

MUNERONI: What's the most exciting aspect of "production dramaturgy"? Perhaps you can draw on a recent experience you had in this field.

REILLY: There are two aspects that I love equally in production dramaturgy. First, there is the initial research period. At this point there have been some preliminary conversations with the director, and perhaps the designers, but very few decisions have been made. In my experience, this is where the dramaturg may have the most influence because everything is still conceptual. In this luxurious window (almost) every idea can be entertained. It can be ridiculously fun, especially when your collaborators are feeling as generous as you are. In their heart of hearts, dramaturges are theatre nerds in the deepest sense of nerdism. This initial phase of the production process is one of the only times ever that I can just "geek out" with other theatre nerds. I always find this phase inspiring.

Most of my dramaturgical experience has been with university theatres, and my second favourite aspect of dramaturgy reflects my career as a theatre history professor. One of the most consistent expectations for production dramaturgs is some kind of historical presentation to the cast at the first table read. I find that this presentation is one of the only times that most undergraduate students give theatre history their full attention. There is almost always an "aha!" moment where students see that the classes that they endure have a place in their creative process. I have had some very satisfying theatre history class sessions, but nothing compares with the table reads that end with cast members taking on the historical narratives of their characters or being moved by the circumstances in which the play that they are embarking on was first produced.

MUNERONI: As a production dramaturg, what kind of research do you usually conduct in preparation for the staging a play? Can you give an example?

REILLY: I am currently serving as the production dramaturg for William Shakespeare's *Richard III*. I started the process with a close textual analysis of the play. Since it is a history play, I have also conducted research into the War of the Roses with the expectation that I will give a presentation at the first table reading with the cast. I have found that these comprise the fundamental activities of the dramaturgical process. In my experience, some productions only carve out this space for dramaturgical support.

Fortunately, my collaborators are very open-minded to the kinds of contributions that a dramaturg may make to the creative process. I don't find that this is always the case, so I am making the most of it. The director has created a 90-minute cutting of the play, and I am serving as his editor for that process. We want to protect the integrity of Shakespeare's text, but need to be expeditious as possible given our largely undergraduate audience. The director and I are co-creating news broadcasts that we will insert between scenes to provide exposition of the complicated history for the audience. Furthermore, the director has conceived of the royal houses (York and Lancaster) as contemporary fashion houses and is setting the play in a near-future landscape of celebrity culture. I need to build a bridge between Shakespeare's play and the director's concept for this production. This has led me to research recent discourse in celebrity image, which I am relating back to Shakespeare's language of self-fashioning.

MUNERONI: Do you think that there is something unique and peculiar to how dramaturgs confront the task of reading a dramatic text?

REILLY: Dramaturgs have an architectural perspective of dramatic texts. When I read a text, it is like walking through an empty building and noting the foundation, the structure, and the details in construction. This is not unlike what directors and designers do, necessarily, but I think for dramaturgs the building is haunted. There are ghosts of the historical past, of previous productions, of plays that have not crossed over. There are sounds coming from outside of things happening in the neighbourhood and the larger culture. And sometimes the director comes in like a poltergeist and starts moving things around in violent or unexpected ways.

MUNERONI: What is it that catches your attention during your first and subsequent readings of a play? What do you write down? Do you take notes?

REILLY: Any text that comes into my hands for a dramaturgical purpose is destroyed by the end of the process. Post-it notes, scribblings, arrows, and diagrams begin to fill its pages immediately. I find the process of "noticing" is very helpful. "What choices have been made here? Why these choices and not others? What difference does it make to my reading to have noticed this?" Framing my reading with these questions tells me a lot about what areas of inquiry to pursue because the questions are often informed by the initial meetings with the production director. I find that when I read the play again, or in a different context, I have very different responses. I think it is the sign of a really good play when the investigation is encouraged time and again.

MUNERONI: Do you have any reading strategies that allow you to tease out the play's given circumstances and characterization?

REILLY: My methodology approaches the play as an economy, or system of resources kept in balance by the playwright's choices (and eventually the directorial choices). For classical plays I use Aristotle's dramatic elements (plot, character, thought, language, music, and spectacle) to tease out the components of the economy. I list these as I go, and use my findings to map out the play's given circumstances and characterization. I find this process keeps me honest in using what the play tells me instead of any preconceived notions the director or I may have about the play.

MUNERONI: As dramaturgs, we are called to hypothesize and make decisions about how/why a play should be staged today. This is an essential aspect of dramaturging and one that speaks directly to how theatre might shed light on relevant sociocultural issues and rejuvenate old stories for new audiences. Can you share your thoughts about this issue, and specifically about your own interest in finding ways to stage plays for contemporary audiences?

REILLY: Theatre making is an agile process for production collaborators. It is part of our training to flex our faculties for critical inquiry and analysis. There are a multitude of ways to approach the production process, and this allows actors, directors, designers, and dramaturgs to have rich, immersive, and very different theatrical experiences. Too often we prescribe a single and stationary role for the audience, and that is to sit quietly and observe the production. We require them to do the heavy lifting when it comes to carrying our storytelling back into the culture. It is critical that we strategize staging plays with contemporary audiences. Even incremental changes in the way that we approach our production process can have multiplying effects for our audiences. Theatre makers need to advocate for changes like opening rehearsals, increasing opportunities for audience feedback, or developing community advisory boards for programming. We are in desperate need of audience development methods with dramaturgical sensibilities.

Works Cited

Blumenfeld, Robert. *Tools and Techniques for Character Interpretation: A Handbook of Psychology for Actors, Writers, and Directors*. Pompton Plains: Limelight Editions, 2006.

Descartes, René. *Meditations on First Philosophy with Selections from the Objections and Replies*. Trans. Michael Moriarty. Oxford: Oxford University Press, 2008.

De Certeau, Michel. *The Practice of Everyday Life*. Berkeley and Los Angeles: University of California Press, 1984.

Lorca, Federico García. *Blood Wedding*. Trans. Ted Hughes. London: Faber and Faber, 1996.

Lorca, Federico García. *Lorca: Three Plays. Blood Wedding, Doña Rosita the Spinster, Yerma*. Trans. Gwynne Edwards and PeterLuke. London: Methuen, 1987.

Lorca, Federico García. *Lorca: Six Major Plays*. Trans. Caridad Svitch. New York: No Passport Press, 2009.

Fo, Dario. *Mistero Buffo: The Collected Plays*. Vol. 2. Trans. by Ron Jenkins. New York: Theatre Communications Group, 2006.

Gerould, Daniel. *Theatre Theory Theatre. The Major Critical Texts from Aristotle and Zeami to Soyinka and Havel*. New York: Applause, Theatre & Cinema Books, 2000.

Loyola, Ignatius. (Trans. George E. Ganss,). *The Spiritual Exercises of Saint Ignatius*. Chicago: Loyola University Press, 1992.

Pinter, Harold. *Old Times*. New York: Grove Press, 1971.

Rabe, David. *Hurlyburly* and *Those the River Keeps*. New York: Grove Press, 1995.

Roudané, Matthew. *Drama Essentials: An Anthology of Plays*. Boston: Houghton Mifflin Company, 2009.

Schultze, Brigitte. "Highways, Byways, and Blind Alleys in Translating Drama: Historical and Systematic Aspects of a Cultural Technique." In *Translating Literatures, Translating Cultures: New Vistas and Approaches in Literary Studies*. Eds. Kurt Mueller-Vollmer and Michael Irmscher. Berlin: Erich Schmidt, 1998.

Shakespeare, William. *Othello*. New York: Quality Paperback Book Club, 1997.

Shepard, Sam. *Seven Plays*. Introduction by Richard Gilman. New York: Bantam Books, 1986.

Stanislavski, Constantin. *An Actor Prepares*. New York: Theatre Arts Books, 1978.

Wooster Group Official Website: http://thewoostergroup.org/twg/twg.php?hamlet

Resources

Degrees with Specific Dramaturgy Programs

Canada

York University

Degree: MFA in Dance choreography and dramaturgy

Website: http://www.yorku.ca/graddanc/mfa/fields.html

Contact Information: Graduate Program in Dance - MFA • 301 Accolade East. 416 736 5137

University of Ottawa

Degree: MA in Theatre Theory and Dramaturgy

Website: http://www.theatre.uottawa.ca/eng/program_masters_theatre.html

Contact Information: Department of Theatre .135 Séraphin-Marion. Room 207. Ottawa ON Canada. K1N 6N5. Tel.: 613-562-5761. Fax: 613-562-5993. theatre@uOttawa.ca

Europe

AARHUS University

Degree: B.c. in Dramaturgy

Website: http://bachelor.au.dk/en/dramaturgy

Contact Information: Nordre Ringgade 1. 8000 Aarhus C. Denmark. +45 8715 0000. au@au.dk

VŠMU, THEATRE FACULTY , ACADEMY OF PERFORMING ARTS BRATISLAVA

Degree: B.c in Directing and Dramaturgy

Website: http://www.df.vsmu.sk/index.php?&do=content. pages.show&main_id=1042

Contact Information: Rector's Academy of Performing Arts in Bratislava. Ventúrska 3, 813 01 Bratislava, Slovakia. Vrátnica 59 30 14 11

Universiteit van Amsterdam

Degree: MA Art and Cultural Studies in Dramaturgy

Website: http://gsh.uva.nl/nl/masters/masterprogramma-s/duale-masters/content/dramaturgie.html

Contact Information: Fanne Boland MA (Master coordinator Dramaturgy). +31 (0) 20 525 8614/2287. fmboland@uva.nl

University of Birmingham

Degree: MPhil Dramaturgy

Website: http://www.dramacentre.bham.ac.uk

Goldsmiths, University of London

Degree: MA in Writing for Performance with a specialist pathway in Dramaturgy

Website: http://www.gold.ac.uk/pg/ma-writing-performance/

Contact Information: Goldsmiths, University of London. New Cross. London SE14 6NW. UK. +44 (0)20 7919 7171

University of Glasgow

Degree: MPhil Dramaturgy

Website: http://www.tfts.arts.gla.ac.uk

Central School of Speech and Drama

Degree: MA Advanced Theatre Practice (Dramaturgy)

Website: http://www.cssd.ac.uk

King College London and RADA:

Degree: MA in Text and Performance Studies

Website: http://www.kcl.ac.uk

University of Kent

Degree: MA in Theatre Dramaturgy

Website: http://www.dramaturgy.org.uk/page2.htm

University of Leeds

Degree: *BA Theatre (Dramaturgy)*

Website: http://www.leeds.ac.uk

University of Nottingham

Degree: MA in Dramaturgy and Performance Analysis

Website: http://www.nottingham.ac.uk

United States

The American Repertory Theatre Institute for Advanced Theatre Training at Harvard University.
Degree: MFA Dramaturgy and Theater Studies Program
Website: http://americanrepertorytheater.org/node/4349
Contact Information: 64 Brattle St. Cambridge, MA 02138
617-496-2000

Carnegie Mellon University, School of Drama
Degree: Bachelor of Arts in Dramaturgy
Website: http://www.drama.cmu.edu/126
Contact Information: SCHOOL OF DRAMA. Purnell Center for the Arts. Carnegie Mellon University. 5000 Forbes Avenue. Pittsburgh, PA 15213

Columbia University
Degree: MFA Dramaturgy Concentration
Website: http://arts.columbia.edu/mfa-dramaturgy-concentration
Contact Information: 601 Dodge Hall Mail. Code 1807 2960. Broadway. New York, NY 10027 Phone: 212-854-3408

Depaul University
Degree: BFA in Dramaturgy
Website: http://theatre.depaul.edu/conservatory/undergraduate/dramaturgy-criticism/Pages/default.aspx
Contact Information: Rachel Shteir. The Theatre School at DePaul University. 2350 N. Racine Ave. Chicago, IL 60614-8422.

Duke University
Degree: Bachelor of Theatre Studies with a focus of Dramaturgy
Website: http://theaterstudies.duke.edu/academics/dramaturgy
Contact Information: Jules Odendahl-James (jao@duke.edu). Box 90680. Durham, NC 27708-0680. 919-660.3343 theater@duke.edu.

San Diego State University

Degree: M.A. in Theatre Arts with Dramaturgy Training

Website: http://theatre.sdsu.edu/index.php/ degree_programs/theatre_MA

Contact Information: School of Theatre, Television and Film. San Diego State University. 5500 Campanile Drive. San Diego, CA 92182-7601. 619-594-5091. aparkhur@mail.sdsu.edu

Stony Brook University

Degree: MFA in Theatre with a Dramaturgy Track

Website: http://www.stonybrook.edu/southampton/mfa/ theatre/index.html

Contact Information: SOUTHAMPTON ARTS. Chancellors Hall. Stony Brook. Southampton. 239 Montauk Highway. Southampton, NY 11968. 631-632-5030

The Ohio State University

Degree: Ph.D in Theatre with Production Training in Dramaturgy

Website: http://theatre.osu.edu/gradstudies/phd

Contact Information: Drake Performance and Event Center. 1849 Cannon Drive. Columbus, Ohio 43210. theatre@osu.edu. 614-292-5821

The University of Arizona, School of Theatre, Film, and Television

Degree: BFA in History and Dramaturgy

Website: http://tftv.arizona.edu/students/areas_of_study/ theatre_studies/bfa_history_dramaturgy

Contact Information: Theatre. P.O. Box 210003. 1025 N Olive Rd. Drama Bldg, Rm 239. Tucson, AZ 85721-0003. THEATRE@ CFA.ARIZONA.EDU. 520-621-7008

University of Iowa

Degree: MFA in Dramaturgy

Website: http://theatre.uiowa.edu/academic-programs/ mfa-programs/dramaturgy

Contact Information: Art Borreca, Head of Dramaturgy. Theatre Arts Department. The University of Iowa. 107 Theatre Building. Iowa City, IA 52242-1705. 319-353-2401 art-borreca@ uiowa.edu

University of Massachusetts, Amherst

Degree: MFA in Dramaturgy

Website: http://www.umass.edu/theater/graduatedramaturg.php

Contact Information: Harley Erdman. harley@theater.umass .edu. Department of Theater, Fine Arts Center 112. University of Massachusetts Amherst. 151 Presidents Drive. Amherst, MA 01003-9331

Yale School of Drama

Degree: MFA and DFA in Dramaturgy and Dramatic Criticism

Website: http://drama.yale.edu/program/dramaturgy-and-dramatic-criticism

Contact Information: Catherine Sheehy. catherine.sheeh@yale .edu. 203-432-1560. Registrar/Admissions Office, Yale School of Drama. 149 York Street. New Haven CT 06511

Works Cited

"A Sampler of Graduate Dramaturgy Programs in the U.S." *American Theatre* 01 2001: 26-8. *ProQuest*. Web. 19 Sep. 2013

http://www.lib.washington.edu/drama/nwtl/playwriting

http://ee.dramaturgy.co.uk/index.php/site/comments/dramaturgy_courses_in_the_uk

http://www.dramaturgy.org.uk/page11.htm

A Bibliography of Play Analysis and Dramaturgy Books

Ball, David. *Backwards & Forwards: A Technical Manual for Reading Plays.* Carbondale: SIU Press, 1984.

Barba, Eugenio. *On Directing and Dramaturgy: Burning the House.* New York: Routledge, 2010.

Barranger, Milly S. *Understanding Plays.* 3rd ed. New York: Pearson, 2003.

Bly, Mark, ed. *The Production Notebooks.* New York: Theatre Communications Group, 1996.

Brockett, Oscar G. "Dramaturgy in Education: Introduction." *Dramaturgy in American Theatre: A Sourcebook* (n.d.): 42. International Bibliography of Theatre & Dance with Full Text.

Brown, Lenora Inez. *The Art of Active Dramaturgy: Transforming Critical Thought into Dramatic Action.* Newburyport, MA: Focus Publishing, 2010.

Burgoyne, Suzanne. *Thinking Through Script Analysis.* Newburyport, MA: Focus Publishing, 2012.

Cardullo, Bert, Ed. *What Is Dramaturgy?* New York: Peter Lang, 1995.

Chemers, Michael Mark. *Ghostlight: An Introductory Handbook for Dramaturgy.* Carbondale, IL: SIU Press, 2010.

Fliotsos, Anne L. *Interpreting the Play Script: Contemplation and Analysis.* New York: Palgrave Macmillan, 2011.

Grote, David. *Script Analysis : Reading and Understanding The Playscript for Production.* Belmont, CA: Wadsworth Pub. Co., 1985.

Hartley, Andrew James. *The Shakespearean Dramaturg: A Theoretical and Practical Guide.* New York: Palgrave MacMillan, 2005.

Ingham, Rosemary. *From Page to Stage: How Theatre Designers Make Connections Between Scripts and Images.* Portsmouth, NH: Heinemann, 1998.

Irelan, Scott, R. Fletcher, Anne, Dubiner, Julie Felise. *The Process of Dramaturgy: A Handbook.* Newburyport, MA: Focus Publishing, 2010.

Kindelan, Nancy. *Shadows of Realism: Dramaturgy and the Theories and Practices of Modernism.* Westport, CT: Praeger, 1996.

Jonas, Susan, Proehl, Geoff, and Lupu, Michael, eds. *Dramaturgy in American Theater: A Source Book.* New York: Harcourt Brace, 1997.

Londré, Felicia Hardison, and Barry Kyle. *Words at Play: Creative Writing and Dramaturgy.* Carbondale, IL: Southern Illinois UP, 2005.

Lennard, John and Luckhurst, Mary, *The Drama Handbook: A Guide to Reading Plays.* Oxford, UK: Oxford University Press, 2002.

Lessing, Gotthold Ephraim, and Julius Petersen. *Lessings Hamburgische Dramaturgie. Hrsg. Und Erläutert Von Julius Petersen.* n.p.: Berlin, Bong & Co., 1916.

Luckhurst, Mary. *Dramaturgy: A Revolution in Theatre.* Cambridge, UK: CUP, 2006.

Martin, Carol. *Dramaturgy of the Real on the World Stage.* Basingstoke, UK: Palgrave Macmillan, 2010.

Milhous, Judith D., and Hume, Robert D., *Producible Interpretation.* Carbondale. IL: Southern Illinois University Press, 1985.

Pritner, Cal, and Walters, Scott. *Introduction to Play Analysis.* New York: McGraw-Hill Humanities, 2004.

Rush, David. *A Student Guide to Play Analysis.* Carbondale, IL: SIU Press, 2005.

Suvin, Darko, *To Brecht and Beyond: Soundings in Modern Dramaturgy.* Brighton, UK: Harvester Press, 1984.

Thomas, James. *Script Analysis for Actors, Directors, and Designers.* 4th ed. Burlington, VT: Focal Press, 2009.

Trencsényi, Katalin, and Cochrane, Bernadette. Eds. *New Dramaturgy: International Perspectives on Theory and Practice.* London: Methuen Drama, 2014.

Turner, Cathy, and Synne K. Behrndt. *Dramaturgy and Performance / Cathy Turner and Synne K. Behrndt.* n.p.: Houndmills, Basingstoke, Hampshire; New York: Palgrave Macmillan, 2008.

Waxberg, Charles S. *The Actor's Script : Script Analysis For Performers.* Portsmouth, NH : Heinemann. 1998.